MODERN DIPLOMATIC LAW

THE MELLAND SCHILL LECTURES
*delivered at the University of Manchester
and published by the University Press*

The Law of International Institutions in Europe
by A. H. Robertson, B.C.L., S.J.D., 1961

The Role of International Law in the Elimination of War
by Professor Quincy Wright, 1961

The Acquisition of Territory in International Law
by Professor R. Y. Jennings, 1962

The Sources and Evidences of International Law
by Clive Parry, LL.D., 1965

Rights in Air Space
by D. H. N. Johnson, M.A., LL.B., 1965

International Law and the Practitioner
by Sir Francis A. Vallat, K.C.M.G., Q.C., 1966

The Law of the Sea
by D. W. Bowett, Ph.D., LL.B., 1967

Modern Diplomatic Law
by Michael Hardy, M.A., LL.M., 1968

International Law and the Uses of Outer Space
by J. E. S. Fawcett, M.A., 1968

OTHER BOOKS IN INTERNATIONAL LAW

Self-Defence in International Law
by D. W. Bowett, Ph.D., LL.B.

Human Rights in Europe
by A. H. Robertson, B.C.L., S.J.D.

The Legal Problems of Foreign Investment in Developing Countries
by E. I. Nwogugu, Ph.D., LL.B.

The Settlement of Boundary Disputes in International Law
by A. O. Cukwurah, Ph.D., LL.B.

Human Rights in National and International Law
edited by A. H. Robertson, B.C.L., S.J.D.

*Legal Aspects of Foreign Investment in
the European Economic Community*
by W. H. Balekjian, Dr. Rer. Pol., Dr. Jur., Ph.D.

MODERN DIPLOMATIC LAW

by

MICHAEL HARDY

M.A., LL.M., Barrister-at-Law

MANCHESTER UNIVERSITY PRESS
U.S.A.: OCEANA PUBLICATIONS INC.

137690.
KW 6

Published by the University of Manchester at
THE UNIVERSITY PRESS
316-324 Oxford Road, Manchester, 13

U.S.A.
OCEANA PUBLICATIONS INC.
75 Main Street, Dobbs Ferry, N.Y. 10522

distributed in India by
N. M. TRIPATHI Private LIMITED
Princess Street, Bombay-2

Library of Congress Catalog Card No. 68–17737

G.B. SBN: 7190 0309 1

Oceana Book No. 23–8

Printed in Great Britain by Butler & Tanner Ltd., Frome and London

FOREWORD

By her Will, the late Miss Olive Schill of Prestbury, Cheshire, an old friend of the University, whose portrait is painted in Lady Katharine Chorley's *Manchester Made Them*, left the sum of £10,000 to the University in memory of her brother, Melland Schill, who died in the 1914–18 war. The annual income from this sum is to be used to promote and publish a series of public lectures of the highest possible standard dealing with International Law.

These lectures by Mr. Michael Hardy on 'Modern Diplomatic Law' have a particular interest, since the entry into force on 24 April 1964 of the Vienna Convention on Diplomatic Relations. For English lawyers in particular, the subject is a practical one, as the Diplomatic Privileges Act, 1964, incorporates Article 1 and Articles 22 to 24 and 27 to 40 of the Convention *expressis verbis* into English law.

Mr. Hardy is a distinguished graduate of the Law Faculties of Oxford and of Cambridge. He has practised at the Bar, taught in the Universities of Manchester and London, and is now a responsible international civil servant on the staff of the Office of Legal Affairs of the United Nations in New York. I hasten to add, however, that the author is merely expressing his own personal views and in no sense intends to commit the United Nations or any other body with which he may be associated to his expression of those views.

B. A. WORTLEY

Faculty of Law,
University of Manchester

CONTENTS

vii

CONTENTS

CONTENTS

ix

Chapter I

ESTABLISHMENT AND FUNCTIONS
OF DIPLOMATIC MISSIONS

INTRODUCTION

It is my aim in these lectures to describe the legal framework of the means by which States pursue their external policies towards one another. I shall not attempt to examine every feature of diplomatic practice or to summarize the pros and cons of all the problems which may arise in the day-to-day life of a diplomatic mission. Nor, even less, will I try to specify what particular policies individual countries have followed and the tactics which should be observed to ensure success. My inquiry goes to the rules and pieces of the game and not to the players and their contests. Accordingly, we shall not be concerned with the widest sense of the word 'diplomacy', where it becomes synonymous with the execution of foreign policy, but with the narrower and more technical use of the word to refer to the means by which a country's foreign relations are maintained. Diplomacy, or diplomatic relations, may be defined for present purposes as being the conduct, through representative organs and by peaceful means, of the external relations of a given subject of international law with any other such subject or subjects. The term 'diplomatic law' therefore comprises the body of legal rules which govern the conduct and status of the organs concerned. The phrase 'through representative organs' refers at once to the delegated and symbolic quality of these organs—to the fact that they are, in short, *agents* whose acts constitute acts on behalf of the parent entity, and to the fact that it is the entity itself which chooses the organ to represent it and the task it shall perform, according to its own internal procedures. 'By peaceful means' excludes war and warlike activities from the sphere of activity of diplomatic agents; in this sense the exercise of diplomatic functions is based on a J. S. Mill-like distinction between the persuasion of others (in which opinion is free) and invasion of their rights (which is entirely forbidden). It is certain, however, that the initiation of direct military measures—for all that diplomacy may have led up to them—excludes the continuance of normal diplomatic relations: *inter arma*

1

silent legates. The clumsy term 'subject of international law' covers the possibility that entities other than States may also engage in diplomatic activities; it includes, therefore, besides the Holy See (in so far as the external relations of that body are insufficiently explained by assimilating it to a national State), the ever-increasing number of inter-governmental organizations with major functions, namely the United Nations, the specialized agencies, the European Communities and the principal regional associations. Each of these, no less than an accepted sovereign State, now acts as a centre of diplomatic representation and is the cause of further diplomatic efforts elsewhere.

Forms of diplomacy

As regards the institutional forms which modern diplomacy may take, States now have at their disposal an unparalleled array of devices for the conduct of their foreign affairs. There is, firstly and primarily, the exchange of permanent diplomatic missions and agents. This institution, which, like so much of the machinery of the modern state system, had its origins in fifteenth-century Italy,[1] has become the commonest form of diplomatic representation; by agreement, two States may exchange envoys and establish an embassy or legation in each other's country. The element of permanence necessarily brings about, by contrast with temporary missions, greater contacts with the law of the receiving State so as to raise the question, in a variety of contexts, of the extent to which the authorities of that State may exercise control over the activities of the foreign envoy and the degree to which they are obliged to respect his immunity from their jurisdiction. The second form of diplomacy consists of missions which may most accurately be described as non-permanent but which are normally referred to as special missions, or *ad hoc* diplomacy. This medium may be divided according to the particular person chosen to conduct the mission or according to the purpose for which the mission is sent, the two matters being usually closely linked. One category consists of visits made or meetings attended by leading political figures, whether heads of State or Government attempting to resolve major political difference, or foreign ministers representing their countries at regular sessions of international organizations.[2] Besides

[1] It may be noted that the dispatch of diplomatic envoys was not an exclusively Western invention: see Sen, *A Diplomat's Handbook of International Law and Practice* (1965), p. 3.
[2] As one former holder of that office has written, 'Today a foreign minister has

2

this class of special missions, conducted by persons having direct political responsibility, there are what may be termed special missions proper. These are composed of persons designated for the particular task or given special rank for the occasion. Besides the traditional example of the appointment of a representative to attend a ceremonial function, such as a coronation or a presidential installation, temporary missions may also be employed for more immediate political or technical purposes. Thus a special mission may be sent to explain a matter of particular delicacy and importance involving a shift in government policy or, since such missions may be used (unlike the case of permanent representation) when the two Governments do not recognize one another, in order to explore the possibility of establishing, or re-establishing, diplomatic relations. The discussion of financial problems, postal arrangements, the exchange of civil aviation facilities, the sharing of hydroelectric power, and a host of kindred matters may also require the dispatch, often for considerable periods, of expert groups possessed, at least within their field of competence, of power to represent their country and, often, to enter into binding agreements.

Special missions are to be distinguished from the official representation of a State at an *ad hoc* conference convened by a particular Government and from state representation in an international organization. The problems relating to the conduct of international conferences summoned by individual States cannot be covered here, except to note that the privileges and immunities accorded by the host State are often the same as those which would be given to members of a special mission dealing with a similar topic. In the case of the major international organizations on the other hand, the possession of an independent legal personality, the establishment of permanent offices at which States may institute missions similar to those accredited to States, the regular nature of the meetings held and the scope of the matters considered, combine to render the forms of diplomatic activity involved sufficiently distinctive and important as to require separate discussion. As in the exchange of permanent missions between States, the element of duration brings with it an increase in the range of possible contacts with the local jurisdiction and a correspondingly greater need for precise regulation of the position of the various parties concerned.

---

on his agenda, at least once or twice a month, a meeting of an international body which he must attend in person.' Beyen, 'Diplomacy by Conference', *Diplomatie unserer Zeit* (ed. Braunas and Stourzh, 1959), p. 63.

This summary of the major forms through which States conduct their external relations shows how varied those means now are; it is a complicated instrument upon which States are allowed to play— now sending a special mission, now exchanging envoys with another State, now preparing for a coming session of one of the principal international bodies. Before describing in more detail the legal issues raised, in particular as regards permanent diplomatic missions and state representation in international organizations, it is necessary to examine the sources and theoretical bases of the legal rules involved.

Sources of diplomatic law

Diplomatic relations are regulated by law for the same reason as many other branches of human activity, namely from a general recognition that only by so doing can affairs be conducted smoothly. The foundation of diplomatic law lies accordingly in the desire of States that their diplomatic relations should function on a stable and orderly basis. Granted the existence of independent, potentially antagonistic, sovereign States, legal regulation provides a feeling of security: it implies, as Bentham said, 'a given extension of future time in respect to all that good which it embraces'.[1] Nevertheless we must remember that we are referring primarily to international law, a system of law unique in the discretion which it leaves to its subjects in the choice and application of given legal rules. Thus, in the particular context of diplomatic law, it must be emphasized that this body of law normally only comes into operation after a State has agreed to accept the representative of another.[2] The position may be summarized by saying that whereas some of the international rules involved in this body of law directly affect States in their relations as executives, others acquire their main relevance within the confines of national law, the major example being, of course, the sphere of diplomatic privileges and immunities. A State is, however, allowed to determine for itself how to give effect to its international obligations. The various national measures taken, including judicial decisions, relating to diplomats, although not sources of law for other States, are accordingly indicative of the understanding of particular States

[1] *The Theory of Legislation* (ed. Ogden, 1931), p. 97.
[2] Thus it may be noted that the Diplomatic Privileges Act 1964, c. 81, adopted to give effect within the United Kingdom to the Vienna Convention on Diplomatic Relations, reproduces less than half the provisions of the Convention (Articles 1, 22–4 and 27–40), those omitted (apart from the final clauses) being directed solely to the executive.

as to the extent of their obligations in international law, and as such evidence of the content of that law.

On the international plane, the sources of diplomatic law are largely to be found (or were, at least, until recently largely to be found) in the customary rules of international law. No general treaty has hitherto existed to which States could adhere, nor have States been required by any formal act to acknowledge their acceptance of the body of rules comprised under the term 'diplomatic law'. In this sphere, if in no other, a 'constant and uniform usage, accepted as law',[1] has emerged, recognized by all States, albeit with some divergence as to the details of its application. To this statement two exceptions exist. Firstly, in a limited number of cases provision has been made by bilateral treaty for the grant of privileges and immunities to the respective envoys of the two States. These treaties,[2] mostly dating from the late nineteenth century, between Latin American and Middle and Far Eastern States on the one hand, and European nations or the United States on the other, are of relatively minor significance; apart from the agreement expressed that the two countries should enter into diplomatic relations and exchange official envoys, the privileges and immunities to be awarded were usually left to be determined according to general international law. The other exception, which is very much more important, concerns the adoption in 1961 of the Vienna Convention on Diplomatic Relations, which regulates in detail the status of permanent diplomatic missions and agents exchanged between States.[3] Although there had been previous attempts to give general regulation to this topic, these had been incomplete either in their results or in the scope of the matters covered. In 1815 the Regulation adopted at the Congress of Vienna settled the previously highly disputed question of rank and precedence among envoys; the League of Nations examined the matter between 1924 and 1928 but, apart from collecting material regarding state practice, did not pursue its inquiries beyond the level of an expert committee;[4] and, in 1928, the Sixth International American Conference which met at Havana adopted a Convention

---

[1] *Asylum Case, I.C.J. Reports, 1950*, p. 277.

[2] These treaties are described and listed in Harvard Law School, *Research in International Law, I: Diplomatic Privileges and Immunities* (1932), p. 26.

[3] The status of special missions may also shortly be regulated by a Convention. See p. 91 below.

[4] The consideration of the topic by the League of Nations is summarized in the Secretariat memorandum, 'Diplomatic Intercourse and Immunities', *Yearbook of the International Law Commission, 1956*, vol. II, pp. 136–46.

regarding Diplomatic Officers, to which a dozen or more Latin American States adhered.[1] Only in the case of the 1961 Convention, however, was the matter carried to a successful conclusion so as to produce a codified version of the existing rules acceptable to the generality of States.[2] To the extent to which the Convention is an exercise in 'pure' codification, namely the consolidation of an already accepted body of customary law, the rules which it embodies are binding *erga omnes*, except in the cases where a State has consistently maintained a contrary practice. It should, however, be noted that the Vienna Convention is not exhaustive in the sense of containing all relevant customary rules, even though it certainly contains most of them. The Preamble to the Convention affirms expressly that 'the rules of customary international law should continue to govern questions not expressly regulated by the provisions of the present Convention'.[3] To the extent to which, on the other hand, the Convention is more than an authoritative statement of existing rules (the

[1] United Nations Legislative Series, *Laws and Regulations regarding Diplomatic and Consular Privileges and Immunities* (1958), vol. VII, p. 419. In so far as the International Law Commission was guided by previous attempts at codification, the Havana Convention and the Draft Convention on Diplomatic Privileges and Immunities, prepared under the auspices of the Harvard Law School, were the most influential. The latter is contained in Harvard Law School, op. cit., p. 19.

[2] The Convention, which was adopted following the United Nations Conference on Diplomatic Intercourse and Immunities held at Vienna between 2 March and 14 April 1961, entered into force on 24 April 1964. The text of the Convention and list of States parties is given in Appendix II, p. 129 below.
The Conference had before it as the basic proposal for its consideration the revised draft articles which the International Law Commission had prepared on the topic in 1958. The Special Rapporteur (Mr. A. E. F. Sandström (Sweden)), who was appointed by the International Law Commission in 1954, submitted a report in 1955 (*Yearbook of the International Law Commission, 1955*, vol. II, p. 9), which was considered by the Commission at its ninth session in 1957. The International Law Commission adopted a provisional set of draft articles with a commentary (*Yearbook of the International Law Commission, 1957*, vol. II, p. 132). This draft was sent to Governments for their comments and discussed in the Sixth Committee during the twelfth session of the General Assembly. In 1958 the International Law Commission examined the text of the provisional draft in the light of the observations made and submitted a revised set of draft articles, and commentary, to the General Assembly (*Yearbook of the International Law Commission, 1958*, vol. II, p. 89). After consideration of the revised draft by the Sixth Committee, the General Assembly decided by resolution 1450(XIV) of 7 December 1959, that a plenipotentiary conference should be convened in order to adopt an international convention on the topic, based on the revised draft articles.

[3] This clause, not contained in the draft prepared by the International Law Commission (which did not include a Preamble) was inserted at the Vienna Conference at the instigation of the Swiss delegation. It constitutes a kind of reservation, or preservation, of the previous law, rather as an English statute might declare that all matters not expressly regulated continue to be governed by common law.

'best evidence' as it were) and introduces new law, a different position obtains, at least in theory, and only those States are bound which have become parties to the instrument without reservation on the point in question. But the distinction between 'pure' codification and 'new' codification is unreal; though it adorns our legal texts it fails to provide a decisive guide. The distinction cannot be drawn with certainty as regards any, or scarcely any, of the provisions; they nearly all partake of old and new, the new consisting, for the most part, not of innovations as such but of resolution of long-standing points of difference in which, to a large degree, it was less important which rule was adopted provided one rule was clearly chosen and followed by all. The question of ratification is also, to a considerable extent, a false issue when presented in overly clear-cut terms. Provided the codification conference has been adequately prepared— and the process whereby the International Law Commission, the Sixth Committee of the United Nations and individual Member States engage in a triangular dialogue has proved, on the whole, remarkably effective for the purpose—the generality of States are likely to endorse the results achieved. If they do, it may be expected that the new instrument will carry away the rest of the pre-existing law with it. The burden of proof resting on non-adhering States to show the existence of a contrary rule or practice, and even on those States maintaining reservations based on custom with respect to given issues, will be very great. In effect, though not legislative in the sense of being formally obligatory on all States, conventions such as those on the law of the sea[1] and the two Vienna Conventions on Diplomatic and Consular Relations[2] move the law on to another level; they henceforth constitute the basis from which discussion starts.

As regards the sources of diplomatic law applicable in the case of international organizations, the position differs in that, from the outset, the basis of the pertinent rules has been conventional.[3] Besides the inclusion in the constitutions of the majority of these organizations of an article referring, in broad terms, to the legal status of representatives, it has been customary for member States to adopt a general instrument, such as the Convention on the Privileges and Immunities of the United Nations[4] and the similar convention

---

[1] See Bowett, *Law of the Sea* (1967).

[2] The Vienna Convention on Consular Relations was adopted in 1963 and came into force on 19 March 1967. The question of consular relations and immunities is not dealt with in the course of the present lectures.

[3] This question is considered more fully on p. 106 ff. below.

[4] Adopted by the General Assembly on 13 February 1946. United Nations

relating to the specialized agencies.[1] In addition agreements have usually been concluded with the States in whose territories permanent offices have been established or where meetings are to be held, setting out the relative entitlements of the host State, of member States, and of the organization. These agreements, together with the internal regulations of the body concerned, have formed the main sources of the law relating to state representatives, with custom and practice following behind to eke out the written provisions.

Theoretical bases of privileges and immunities

Having separated the main sources of diplomatic law it is necessary to look further into the manner of operation of that law. A major portion of diplomatic law is concerned with the action of States in their capacity as executives; the decision to exchange diplomatic missions, the choice of individual representatives, or the ruling that a given envoy is no longer *persona grata*, for example, are not matters which require national legislation in order to achieve their effects or which may be brought before the courts for review. These aspects depend on the exercise of the political discretion left to the executive of sovereign States, whether the particular action is one taken unilaterally or in conjunction with another Government. Even in the case of relations between States and international organizations where an additional element is introduced, a distinction may be drawn between matters regulated on an inter-governmental plane and those whose main operation is in terms of national law.[2] The rules and topics dealt with primarily between executives are accordingly to be distinguished from those which become applicable within the receiving State after the decision has been made by the Government to accept an envoy or, in the case of an international organization, after a state representative has been dispatched in accordance with the rules of the organization and any relevant agreements.

The duty which the receiving State owes under international law as regards the inviolability of diplomatic premises and the jurisdictional immunity of foreign representatives is definite enough; the

---

Legislative Series, *Legislative Texts and Treaty Provisions concerning the Legal Status, Privileges and Immunities of International Organizations* (1959), vol. I, p. 184.

[1] Approved by the General Assembly on 21 November 1947. United Nations Legislative Series, op. cit. (1961), vol. II, p. 101.

[2] Particular considerations may apply with respect to relations between a State and an international organization, but since no organization maintains a municipal legal system similar to that of a State the distinction drawn in the text remains applicable.

manifestation of that duty, however, is to be found in a municipal context. Although, therefore, in the event of a breach of the duty, the sending State may have recourse through diplomatic channels to an official protest, and even possibly the submission of a claim for reparation, the measures which the receiving State may take beforehand will be internal, directed to its organs and citizens. The receiving State is required to ensure that the standards set by international law are met and may employ for the purpose whatever means or combination of means it chooses, whether administrative, legislative or judicial. This entails, as the case may be, the provision of adequate police protection for diplomatic premises; the furnishing of instructions to officials regarding the treatment to be given to diplomatic agents; the submission by the executive of statements to local courts certifying that diplomatic premises and personnel are not subject to jurisdiction; and, as regards the adoption of legislation, the exemption of the representatives of other Governments from the application of certain laws and the imposition of special penalties on citizens who violate the physical safety of foreign envoys.

These restrictions, self-imposed or selected in their details, go to make up that body of international and national law known as diplomatic privileges and immunities.[1] Three explanations have been offered as to why this bundle of rules, constituting the particular legal status enjoyed by diplomatic missions and agents in foreign countries, should exist. The first, originally developed by Grotius, is that of the exterritoriality of the diplomat and of embassy premises.[2] As regards diplomatic premises, all acts performed in the building are regarded, or were regarded, as being performed in the country represented, so as to fall within the latter's jurisdiction and not in that of the actual host State. In the case of the diplomat himself, this image or analogy applied less clearly. However, by the use of the maxim *par in parem non habet imperium* and by stressing the notion that the diplomat represented, and indeed stood as a direct substitute for, the sovereign

---

[1] The word 'privilege' is sometimes used to denote a benefit over and above that ordinarily granted by national law (e.g. in respect of communications) and 'immunity' to describe an exemption from a specific provision of local law (e.g. immunity from taxation), but there is no uniformity of usage and much difficulty in applying the terms consistently with these meanings. Throughout the present lectures the words 'privilege' and 'immunity' are therefore used as synonyms.

[2] See Simmonds, 'Privilèges diplomatiques et naissance de la fiction de l'exterritorialité', *Revue de droit international et droit comparé*, xxxvi (1959), p. 170, showing how Grotius incorporated and superseded the 'representational' theories developed by his predecessors before the notion of territorial jurisdiction had been fully developed.

who sent him, it was possible to extend to the envoy the benefits of being judged solely by his sovereign's law, even as regards acts performed outside the embassy. The limits of this explanation are obvious. The premises of an embassy are situated and the duties of an envoy are actually carried out within the territory of the receiving State. Although for many purposes the authority of the sending State is supreme within the embassy, and the sending State alone determines how its personnel shall be employed, this is not to say that the law of the territorial State is entirely excluded. The very title to the land on which the embassy is situated, or even the claim to occupation of the buildings, must be construed in terms of local law —let alone such questions as whether crimes, possibly unconnected with diplomatic functions, committed by local nationals in embassy premises, are to be judged by the law of the sending State. Furthermore, although the diplomat may have immunity from jurisdiction, it cannot be seriously argued that every act performed by him is to be regarded as *extra territorium*, as though he were the walking embodiment of a system of conflict of laws. If a diplomat buys a newspaper at the corner of the street or orders a meal it may be that he cannot be sued on the contract, but that is not to say that the law governing the transaction is not that of the host State. By its very excesses, the exterritoriality principle is inadequate to explain why certain immunities from local law are accorded. There is a fictional element in this approach which the modern mind finds hard to accept; it is a crutch, helpful to an earlier age, but which we are deemed mentally robust enough to do without. And this is, indeed, the case. There are relatively few modern judgements which base themselves upon this doctrine, or textbooks either. The dismissal by the International Law Commission[1] of this rationale, following a similar rejection by the League of Nations expert committee,[2] may be taken as conclusive.

The remaining explanations, based on the representational qualities of the diplomat and the functional necessities of his office, are not so much opposed as complementary. The original version of the 'representative character' theory identified the envoy with the sovereign so as to exempt him from the jurisdiction of the receiving State by virtue of the status of his master. This interpretation did not accord, however, with the fact that a diplomat's privileges and immunities with regard to local law are not identical, and may indeed be more extensive, than those enjoyed by an individual ruler; nor, even in a

[1] *Yearbook of the International Law Commission, 1958*, vol. II, p. 95.
[2] *American Journal of International Law* (1926), Supplement, p. 149.

revised form, does it account for the problem of equal sovereignties: if both receiving and sending States are sovereign, why should one yield to the other? Nevertheless the theory does stress the all-important fact that the legal status enjoyed by a diplomatic agent is based on his quality as the representative of an independent State, and the belief that relations between such States will be aided by giving representatives an assured freedom of action. The 'functional necessity' theory, which declares that the diplomat receives the privileges and immunities requisite to enable him to perform his task, and for that reason only, is the modern one, and seems to solve the problem in suitably aseptic fashion. But how far does it solve the problem really?—a kitchen stool and a baroque throne are equally functional in their way. Whilst the 'functional necessity' test represents a return to basic principles and to what in this connexion Montesquieu called, *'la raison, tirée de la nature de la chose'*,[1] to learn what the functional criterion amounts to one must refer once more to what is represented, namely a State, and not just to the details of the diplomat's daily occupation. The representational and the functional theories are therefore to be found yoked together in the Preamble to the Vienna Convention, in the following format:

... the purpose of ... privileges and immunities is not to benefit individuals but to ensure the efficient performance of the functions of diplomatic missions as representing States.[2]

The chief importance of the functional explanation lies in its shift of emphasis; it indicates the way in which States have sought to move away from the assumption that immunities might be demanded

---

[1] *De l'esprit des lois* (1748), livre 26, ch. XXI.

[2] The legislative history of this provision is of some interest. Despite the arguments of some members, in particular those of Mr. Tunkin (USSR), the International Law Commission opted mainly for the 'functional necessity' test, while also acknowledging the 'representative character' theory. At the Vienna Conference itself the words 'as representative organs of State' were added at the suggestion of Mr. Tunkin, in his capacity as delegate of the USSR (*United Nations Conference on Diplomatic Intercourse and Immunities, Official Records*) (subsequently referred to as *Official Records*), vol. I, pp. 227 and 229), to an Afro-Asian amendment (A/CONF.20/C.1/L.329), referring only to the efficient performance of functions by missions. After drafting changes the clause was adopted in the form quoted, which thus links the two matters of function and representational quality.

The written proposals and amendments put forward at the Vienna Conference are contained in *Official Records*, vol. II; those submitted to the Committee of the Whole have the symbol A/CONF.20/C.1/L., followed by a serial number, while those submitted to the Plenary Conference begin with the symbol A/CONF.20/L.

automatically on a plea of 'sovereignty', to the notion that the question whether or not privileges are to be accorded is one which is subject to re-assessment in the light of practical needs. It is therefore particularly apposite as regards state representation in international organizations,[1] whilst in the case of purely bilateral relations it buttresses the position of the receiving State without unduly diminishing that of the sending State. In submitting their claims for consideration based on this ground, moreover, individual parties are required to acknowledge their interest, in common with others, in the operation of diplomatic functions. Nevertheless, although some functional limitations have been introduced in modern diplomatic law with respect to specified categories of staff, the difficulty of grading every immunity to every diplomat and, above all, the reluctance of States, *qua* sending States, to allow their fellows, *qua* receiving or host States, to be the judge of what privileges and immunities should be accorded in individual instances, have prevented the functional test from being applied as rigorously as its postulates suggest.

Having laid down this keynote, the practical issues remain. What in fact are the privileges and immunities to be provided in given cases? What importance is to be attached to the fact that whereas in some, perhaps most cases, the local courts would be capable of determining the matter were it not for the personal immunity enjoyed by the defendant, in others they lack competence by reason of the nature of the act performed? How does international law in fact determine the ordering of priorities between the interests of the receiving and of the sending State? In essence it is with this last question that the Vienna Convention on Diplomatic Relations is concerned. In the ensuing lectures I shall deal, firstly and mainly, with the Vienna Convention so as to show how the rules established under that instrument operate, one with another, in a way which ensures that permanent diplomatic missions may function effectively between States. After considering the Vienna Convention, I shall describe, in brief terms, the legal status of special missions. Lastly, I shall examine the question of representation at international organizations.

---

[1] See Convention on the Privileges and Immunities of the United Nations, Article IV, Section 14.

ESTABLISHMENT OF DIPLOMATIC RELATIONS
AND OF DIPLOMATIC MISSIONS[1]

The entry into an agreement to establish diplomatic relations is an act of political discretion which rests in the hands of the two executives concerned. Internationally no special requirement must be fulfilled before the agreement can come into effect other than that the two Governments should recognize one another, a prerequisite which is in any case satisfied by the decision to enter into diplomatic relations. Nor do provisions of internal law normally prescribe the conditions which must be met before this discretion may be used, although constitutional statutes commonly specify the organ which is to exercise the power in question. Externally, although other States may consider it desirable, or undesirable, that two countries should enter into relations with one another, they cannot do more than offer advice to this effect; steps beyond this would constitute interference in the affairs of the State in question.[2] The Vienna Convention leaves the establishment of diplomatic missions, like the institution of diplomatic relations, to be governed by the consent of the two States concerned, without attempting to direct in any way when that consent should be exercised or refused.[3] The 'right of legation' is thus more

[1] Here and elsewhere the term 'diplomatic mission' refers to permanent diplomatic missions sent between one State and another, and not to special missions or those maintained at international organizations.

[2] On this ground the General Assembly could not, it was said, enjoin Greece to establish diplomatic relations with Albania and Bulgaria, as proposed in a draft resolution put forward by the USSR (A/C.1/623). The most the General Assembly could do was to counsel Greece to resume relations, as it had done in resolution 288A(IV) of 18 November 1949. See the statement of the Representative of France, *Official Records of the General Assembly*, Fifth Session, First Committee, 395th meeting, 13 November 1950, p. 319.

[3] There were several attempts during the proceedings in the International Law Commission and at the Vienna Conference to gain endorsement of the 'right' of all States to send and receive envoys. The original proposal of the Special Rapporteur referred to States 'ayant le droit de légation' (Article 1, *Yearbook of the International Law Commission*, 1955, vol. II, p. 10). This raised the question of which entities possessed the right of legation, and whether the determination was to be made by the would-be sending State or by the intended receiving State. Assuming the right to exist, was it accompanied by an obligation on other States to receive the envoys sent? If it was subject to consent (as all were agreed) what was the force of the 'right'? In the light of these considerations the International Law Commission decided to make no reference to the right in its draft. At the Conference a Czech proposal (A/CONF.20/C.1/L.7), declaring that every State possesses the right of legation, was withdrawn after a number of Afro-Asian delegates had expressed opposition on the ground that it would render the text too 'aggressive' (Delegate of Tunisia, *Official Records*, vol. I, p. 78).

13

correctly to be regarded, in Hohfeldian terms, as an accordable liberty rather than as a *de jure* attribute of every sovereign State accompanied by a corresponding obligation on the part of the selected partner. In this respect, as in a significant number of others, the position of individual nations remains as it has been since the emergence of the modern state system: legally, each State is free to determine, in a series of bilateral agreements and normally on condition of reciprocity, the existence and extent of its relations with any other State; in practical terms no State is able to maintain its position without sending and receiving envoys on an increasing scale.

The actual agreement between the two States expressing their willingness to enter into diplomatic relations may be in the form of a solemn treaty or may be more informal—an exchange of notes between foreign ministers, between ambassadors stationed in a third country, or perhaps between United Nations representatives following discussions at foreign minister level held during a session of the General Assembly. The agreement, of indefinite duration, may be ended on the determination by either side that the premises originally underlying the agreement no longer prevail—in other words, a right of unilateral appraisal of the principle of *rebus sic stantibus*. Although the other State may object to the action taken as being markedly 'unfriendly' or based on a wrong assessment of the facts, it will rarely be able, or even attempt, to claim that the State wishing to end diplomatic relations is under an obligation not to do so.[1] In the case of the mission itself, the sending State may decide, without going so far as to break off diplomatic relations, to recall its mission, either permanently or temporarily. It may, in this event, entrust a third State with the custody of mission premises and property, and the protection of its interests and those of its nationals, subject, however, to the State which is chosen being acceptable to the receiving State.[2]

[1] In one of the few cases in which such a claim was put forward, the USSR protested to the League of Nations in 1936 that the action of Uruguay in suspending diplomatic relations, on the ground that the Soviet Mission in Montevideo had been involved in subversive activities in a neighbouring country, was a violation of Article XII(1) of the Covenant requiring Member States to submit disputes likely to lead to a rupture to specified forms of settlement. Uruguay's right to take action was upheld by the Council of the League: the requirements of the Article were not intended to place States under an obligation to maintain diplomatic relations irrespective of the circumstances. In the resolution adopted on 24 January 1936 the Council expressed the hope that the two States would resume diplomatic operations at a favourable opportunity and would refrain from acts which might be harmful to the interests of peace. Hyde, 'Freedom to Withdraw Diplomatic Relations', *American Journal of International Law*, 30 (1936), p. 471,

[2] Article 45(*b*) and (*c*).

As these examples make clear, the fundamental agreement to enter into diplomatic relations and to establish a permanent mission constitutes the basis or, as the French phrase more aptly puts it, *l'accord cadre*, for a number of further agreements or unilateral acts designed to regulate supplementary matters. Some of these, such as the appointment of certain members of the staff, the installation of offices away from the seat of the mission and the grant of privileges and immunities over and above those contained in the Convention, require the consent of both States. Many issues, however, are left to the sole determination of one or other State, including, so far as the sending State is concerned, the range of tasks to be performed by individual members of the staff in execution of the functions of the mission as a whole.

FUNCTIONS OF DIPLOMATIC MISSIONS

Normal functions

As regards the choice of the functions which a permanent mission may perform—an issue which one might think central to diplomatic law—no precise definition exists or has been evolved. Books describing diplomatic practice give an account of the kind of tasks in which diplomats have traditionally been engaged, with some paragraphs added concerning more recent developments, such as the promotion of trade and relations with the press and general public. But how far may these activities extend? What activities are extra-legal? If a State agrees to receive a permanent mission is it bound to allow the performance of the entire range of possible diplomatic functions or may it prohibit certain activities? Broadly speaking, the answer to these questions is that there is a reasonably well-established core of meaning describing the standard functions of a permanent mission, and the consent of a State to receive a mission is deemed to denote its consent that the mission shall perform at least those functions which fall within the usual pattern. Beyond the accepted cases there is a certain area, unspecified in extent, in which States are left to settle the matter by negotiation and mutual agreement. The Vienna Convention gives a loose definition, distinguishing the five main functions of a diplomatic mission in the following terms:

The functions of a diplomatic mission consist, *inter alia*, in:
    (*a*) Representing the sending State in the receiving State;
    (*b*) Protecting in the receiving State the interests of the sending State and of its nationals, within the limits permitted by international law;
    (*c*) Negotiations with the Government of the receiving State;

15

(*d*) Ascertaining by all lawful means conditions and developments in the receiving State, and reporting thereon to the Government of the sending State;

(*e*) Promoting friendly relations between the sending State and the receiving State, and developing their economic, cultural and scientific relations.[1]

The representational character of the mission's functions, referred to in sub-paragraph (*a*) is a generic description which could be used to cover each of the other tasks mentioned. The protection of the interests and nationals of the sending State, the conduct of negotiations, and the ascertaining of information about the receiving State, constitute the three traditional aspects of an ambassador's work. The references to the promotion of friendly relations and the development of economic, cultural and scientific ties reflects more recent preoccupations. It is, at all events, on the bedrock of this provision that many of the subsequent articles depend; indeed, despite the non-exhaustive character of the definition given, an assumed understanding of what the functions of a mission consist of runs like a ghostly *leitmotif* through the machinery of the Convention. References are made, expressly or by implication, throughout the instrument to the official acts of mission staff or to the performance of the work of the mission as a whole, which receive explanation only in the light of the general provision cited above. Having regard also to the reliance placed on the doctrine of functional necessity, as one of the underlying bases for the enjoyment of privileges and immunities, the question of the scope of the functions of a mission and of its members may become of major importance in cases placed before the courts, no less than in those which become the subject of diplomatic correspondence.

Consular functions

Besides the functions of a solely diplomatic character which it may perform, a permanent mission may also carry out consular activities. This question, which is dealt with obliquely in Article 3, caused considerable debate at the Conference itself since a number of States, in particular the Soviet Union, wished the Convention to provide that diplomatic missions might automatically perform consular tasks, whilst others, whose main spokesman was the Spanish delegate, wanted to give the receiving State the power to say yes or no. The wording selected is deliberately non-committal:[2] the conduct of con-

[1] Article 3, paragraph 1.

[2] 'Nothing in the present Convention shall be construed as preventing the performance of consular functions by a diplomatic mission.' Article 3, paragraph 2.

sular functions by diplomatic missions is not prohibited by the Convention, but neither is it expressly authorized; the end result is that the receiving State may continue to demand, if it wishes to do so, that its consent be obtained before such functions are conducted, but the sending State has some basis on which to rely in arguing that consular activities form part of the accepted range of functions of a permanent mission. Since the adoption of the Vienna Convention on Diplomatic Relations, the matter has been carried a stage further by the entry into force on 19 March 1967 of the Vienna Convention on Consular Relations, Article 2, paragraph 2, of which provides that consent to the establishment of diplomatic relations implies consent to consular relations also. In view of the difficulty of distinguishing many diplomatic tasks—for example, the protection of nationals and the promotion of trade—from those performed by consuls, and the tendency in many countries to merge diplomatic and consular staff into a single foreign service, this clarification is to be welcomed.

Extraordinary functions

The matters dealt with above concern the normal exercise of diplomatic functions on a bilateral basis. In three contingencies, however —namely in the event of the rupture of diplomatic relations, the recall of a mission, or the simple absence of diplomatic relations— a State may entrust the protection of its interests and those of its nationals to a third State, or, as the case may be, itself be entrusted with responsibility for the protection of the interests of a third State. In each instance the consent of the receiving State is required.[1]

Manner of exercise of functions

The conditions under which the functions of a mission may be performed is dealt with in Article 41 of the Convention. Besides providing that all persons enjoying privileges and immunities are required to respect the laws and regulations of the receiving country, it is expressly stated that such persons 'have a duty not to interfere in the internal affairs of that State'. This provision embraces, besides private acts, activities which the sending State may sanction and, indeed, officially order the diplomat to execute, although they constitute, in the eyes of the receiving State, acts of gross interference in its internal affairs.

A basic guideline as regards the manner in which the affairs of the

---

[1] Articles 45 and 46.

mission are to be performed is provided by the second paragraph of Article 41, which states that

All official business with the receiving State entrusted to the mission by the sending State shall be conducted with or through the Ministry for Foreign Affairs of the receiving State or such other ministry as may be agreed.

In principle, therefore, the foreign ministry of the receiving State is the sole channel through which the functions of the mission are to be executed unless it has been agreed that the mission or its staff members (such as commercial or service attachés) may have direct contacts with other government departments.[1] Such contacts are in fact extremely common and the main purpose of the provision is not so much to maintain, Canute like, the former monopoly over external affairs enjoyed by the foreign ministry—for it was fully recognized that the specialized matters being dealt with by Governments could no longer be handled solely by that means—but to ensure that so far as possible a Government presents a unified viewpoint and is protected against the problems which might arise if a foreign mission were allowed unlimited contact with different branches of the Government, and, indeed, with the country at large.

One issue which, despite its undoubted importance as part of the present-day 'official business' of diplomatic missions, has received little attention in this connexion concerns the propaganda efforts undertaken, either under tacit agreement with the receiving State or as a result of a more formal exchange of views. In 1956, for example, a question was raised in the House of Commons about letters sent by embassies in London to members of the House containing severe criticisms of certain actions and policies of the British Government. In his reply the Under-Secretary of State for Foreign Affairs declared that foreign missions were entitled to circulate propaganda material provided it did not constitute a 'breach of diplomatic privilege'; what the limits of privilege are in this context was not stated.[2]

---

[1] See generally on this topic, Blix, 'The Right of Diplomatic Missions and Consulates to Communicate with Authorities of the Host State', *Scandinavian Studies in Law 1964*, 8, p. 9.

[2] Lauterpacht, 'Contemporary Practice of the United Kingdom', *International and Comparative Law Quarterly*, 6 (1957), p. 318. The reply to a similar question given by the French Foreign Minister placed the accent, more correctly it is considered, on the principle of non-interference in the internal affairs of the receiving State, as well as on that of reciprocity. See Kiss, *Répertoire de la pratique française en matière de droit international public* (1965), tome III, no. 224, pp. 138-9.

Chapter II

STAFF AND FACILITIES OF DIPLOMATIC MISSIONS

APPOINTMENT OF STAFF

ONE of the principal and most original features of the Vienna Convention is the importance it attaches to the institution of the diplomatic mission itself, as an independent entity in its own right. Of permanent duration, enjoying separate privileges and immunities, the mission gives cohesion and organic unity to the acts of the individual persons who, over the years, form its staff. If the ambassador has in this respect lost some of his primary significance, as his new generic title 'head of the mission' suggests, he and the other members of the staff nevertheless remain of direct importance for the execution of the mission's tasks. The Convention divides the personnel of diplomatic missions into three categories: diplomatic agents; administrative and technical staff; and service staff. The first class comprises all those (including the head of mission himself) of diplomatic rank—counsellors, diplomatic secretaries and attachés. The remaining groups consist of the subordinate personnel—on the one hand, the clerical assistants, the archivists and wireless technicians, and, on the other, the drivers, receptionists, maintenance men, and so forth. Although the appointment of other members of the staff can be dealt with in a uniform manner, the distinctive features which attach to the post of head of mission, especially as regards the process of accreditation, require separate description.

Heads of mission

(a) *Agrément and commencement of functions.* The appointment of the head of a diplomatic mission requires an initial act of selection on the part of the would-be sending State, usually exercised by the executive power.[1] The receiving State, having been informed of the name and

---

[1] In the United States ambassadors are nominated by the President 'by and with the Advice and Consent' of the Senate under Article II, Section 2, of the Constitution. See *In re De la Baume*, *Annual Digest*, 1933–4, p. 377, for a successful action brought before the *Conseil d'Etat* by a civil servants' association after

relevant particulars of the person chosen, must then give its consent to his accreditation: until this consent has been obtained the appointment cannot take effect.[1] The need to secure the consent, or *agrément*, of the receiving State is justified by the difficulty and confidential nature of the tasks which the head of the mission may undertake; the appointment of a man who, for some reason, however insignificant or baseless, is not fully acceptable to the receiving State might therefore lead to a worsening of relations between the two States. Although the potential sending State may on occasions be offended or consider the refusal of the receiving State to grant its *agrément* unjustified, no serious movement developed during the discussions in the International Law Commission or at the Vienna Conference to require the receiving State to give its reasons for withholding consent. The text adopted provides expressly that the receiving State is under no obligation in this respect,[2] thus leaving the matter solely to the discretion of the State concerned. If the receiving State decides after it has given its consent that, upon further reflection or in the light of subsequent information, the envoy designated would not be suitable, it may inform the sending State accordingly. This use of this *persona non grata* procedure is, however, distinct from a refusal to grant *agrément* although the net result may be the same in cases where the head of mission has not yet taken up his post.

The procedure for determining the moment at which, and procedure by which, the head of the mission is considered to have taken up his functions is carefully regulated in the Convention. Although much of the importance formerly attached to this issue has diminished, questions of precedence and seniority no longer being as important as they were, the need for a definite rule has not vanished entirely. The matter is indeed almost a textbook example of a situation in which the choice between alternative forms of the rule is less important than agreement on a settled procedure. Article 13 provides that the head of the mission is considered to have taken up his functions either when he has presented his credentials[3] to the head

---

the French Foreign Minister appointed a man who lacked the qualified service required under French administrative law.

[1] Article 4, paragraph 1.

[2] Article 4, paragraph 2.

[3] Credentials, the document officially attesting that the person named is the duly appointed envoy accredited by the sending State to the receiving State, are signed either by the head of State, the head of Government, or by the foreign minister. In the case of high commissioners exchanged between members of the Commonwealth of Nations, the formal document is replaced by a letter of introduction

of State (or, in the case of a chargé d'affaires, to the foreign minister), or when he has notified his arrival and presented a true copy of his credentials to the foreign ministry.[1] The receiving State may decide for itself which procedure shall be followed but must ensure that the practice chosen is applied in the same manner to all representatives. Lest there should be any dispute between different heads of mission arriving within a short span of time, paragraph 2 of Article 13 further specifies that the order of presentation of credentials, or a true copy thereof, is to be determined by the actual date and time of arrival. In this way a firm, if somewhat elaborate, rule exists to mark the moment in time when, by bringing the document certifying his official quality to the notice of the receiving State, a head of mission is deemed to have taken up his functions.[2]

If the post of head of mission becomes vacant or its occupant is unable to perform his functions, a chargé d'affaires ad interim may be appointed as provisional head of mission. In this event no *agrément* is required; the foreign ministry of the receiving State is merely notified of the name of the temporary replacement.[3]

(b) *Classes and precedence.* The fact that heads of missions are divided into different classes is largely a reflection of diplomatic history. During the seventeenth and eighteenth centuries, when the sending of permanent envoys first became customary, no rule existed to determine the order of precedence between representatives sent to the same court. By reason of the superior status of his sovereign, of family relationship between rulers, or by use of a more resounding title (e.g. 'ambassador extraordinary', as opposed to 'ordinary'), each representative sought to advance his claim to prior consideration. Ambassadors returned home if they were not given the *pas* to

---

signed by the prime minister of the sending State, addressed to the head of Government of the receiving State.

[1] Or 'such other ministry as may be agreed', an amendment made to cover the existence of the Commonwealth Office and similar departments.

[2] This question is distinct from that of the moment in time when entitlement to privileges and immunities begins; see p. 80 below.

[3] Article 19, paragraph 1. If no member of diplomatic rank is present in the receiving State, a member of the administrative and technical staff may, if the receiving State gives its consent, be placed in charge of the current administrative affairs of the mission: Article 19, paragraph 2.

The post of chargé d'affaires ad interim (referred to in Article 19, paragraph 1, and Article 5, paragraph 2), which may be filled by any member of the diplomatic staff, should be distinguished from that of a chargé d'affaires accredited to a minister for foreign affairs as a permanent head of mission (Article 14, paragraph 1(c)).

which they considered themselves entitled, and diplomatic relations between the two States might be suspended or even broken off if the insult was grave. To put an end to such disputes a 'Regulation' was adopted at the Congress of Vienna in 1815, later supplemented by a Protocol signed at Aix-la-Chapelle in 1818, dividing representatives into four classes.[1] The first class, which alone was declared to have representative character, consisted of ambassadors, legates and papal nuncios. This category was followed by two further classes of persons accredited to sovereigns, namely envoys and others of similar rank, and ministers resident, and then by the class of chargé d'affaires accredited to ministers of foreign affairs. Precedence was henceforth governed by classes and, within classes, by seniority of appointment at the particular capital.

The main question for the International Law Commission and for the Vienna Conference was that of deciding to what extent this classification should be retained or abandoned. The original draft put forward by the Special Rapporteur suggested that the classes should be reduced to two, those, such as ambassadors, accredited to heads of State, and chargés d'affaires accredited to foreign ministers.[2] Although there was support for this rationalization the reasons against finally held the day. Despite the extensive 'levelling up' in the proportion of ambassadors appointed,[3] a number of States still continue to appoint persons with the rank of envoy or minister. Exclusion of these classes would therefore have had administrative repercussions for the foreign services of the States concerned, and this in turn might have created an obstacle to ratification of the Convention. The pressure for revision was further reduced by the agreement reached that all heads of mission, irrespective of their class, had a representative character and were to be treated equally except as regards matters of precedence and etiquette.[4] On the basis of the Vienna Regulation of 1815 the opinion became widely held during the nineteenth century that only the major powers might exchange ambassadors and, since only the members of this class had a representative character, they alone had the right to demand an audience

[1] The text of the Regulation is reproduced in *Yearbook of the International Law Commission, 1958*, vol. II, p. 93, n. 29, and that of the Aix-la-Chapelle Protocol in *Yearbook of the International Law Commission, 1957*, vol. II, p. 136, n. 7.

[2] Article 7, *Yearbook of the International Law Commission, 1955*, vol. II, p. 10.

[3] For a comparative table showing the practice of a number of countries see J. Salmon, 'Quelques remarques sur les classes des chefs de missions diplomatiques en Belgique', *Revue belge de droit international*, 1 (1965), pp. 172–3.

[4] Article 14, paragraph 2.

with the head of State.[1] The International Law Commission determined that such a right, if it existed, belonged to all heads of mission, and was not to be regarded as a mere matter of etiquette.[2]

As regards the actual text of the 1961 Convention, Article 14 divides heads of mission into three classes:

(a) ambassadors or nuncios accredited to Heads of State, and other heads of mission of equivalent rank;[3]

(b) envoys, ministers and internuncios accredited to Heads of State; and

(c) chargés d'affaires accredited to Ministers for Foreign Affairs.

Thus the only class formally excluded is that of 'ministers resident', introduced by the 1818 Protocol.

The choice of the class to which the head of mission may be assigned in any given case is left to the determination of the States concerned. Although commonly of equal rank, there is no obligation in this respect. Furthermore, even if nominally members of the same class, the two representatives may differ widely in their position in their respective hierarchies; for a small country, the post of ambassador to the nearest great power will be a major appointment, normally held only at the end of a long career, but the same will not apply in the reverse case.

As regards the question of precedence, heads of mission are ranked in their respective classes 'in the order of the date and time of taking up their functions in accordance with Article 13', unless subsequently raised to a higher class by a change in credentials.[4] The only exception to this rule concerns the position of the representative of the Holy See.[5] In accordance with established practice, the receiving State may

---

[1] Martens, *Le Guide diplomatique* (1838), tome I, pp. 43, 54.

[2] *Yearbook of the International Law Commission, 1958*, col. I, p. 125. The advantages of the rank of ambassador for securing access to leading personalities of the receiving State was one of the main reasons given by the Swiss Federal Council in recommending that Switzerland (which had long held out) should follow the practice of appointing agents in the first class: 'ce n'est pas toujours aux bouts de table que s'établissent les contacts les plus utiles!' Message of 5 December 1955 of the Swiss Federal Council, cited in *Annuaire suisse de droit international*, XIII (1956), pp. 169–75.

[3] The latter phrase is intended to cover high commissioners exchanged between members of the Commonwealth of Nations, a number of whom have the same head of State, and high representatives exchanged between members of the French Community. In addition the representative of the Holy See indicated that the term might include papal legates: *Official Records*, vol. I, p. 119.

[4] Article 16, paragraphs 1 and 2.

[5] Article 16, paragraph 3. In a series of bilateral treaties between France and a number of countries formerly under French jurisdiction it is provided that the French representative shall be dean of the diplomatic corps in the States in

give precedence over all other representatives to the representative of the Holy See, who will accordingly act as dean of the local diplomatic corps[1] irrespective of the date of his entry into functions. Although complaints were made that this customary rule was an anachronism and contrary to the principle that all sending States should be treated alike, it enjoyed wide support at the Conference. In the case of members of the diplomatic staff other than the head of mission, the order of precedence is that selected by the sending State and notified to the authorities of the receiving State.[2]

(c) *Plurality of functions.* The head of a mission may be given functions which fall outside the framework of relations exclusively between two States. Provided none of the receiving States objects, a sending State may accredit a head of mission or assign a member of the diplomatic staff to more than one State.[3] Objections raised by some of the smaller States on grounds of the difficulty and administrative inconvenience of obtaining the consent or *nihil obstat* of each receiving State, a requirement at variance with previous international practice, were met by references to the delicate nature of diplomatic relations and the undesirability of presenting receiving States with a *fait accompli.* These considerations were given less weight in the case of the appointment of a head of mission or other diplomatic agent as a representative of the sending State to an international organization.[4] Although France, supported by Switzerland, sought to make such appointments subject to the failure of the receiving State to object, this view failed to receive the necessary majority at the Conference.[5]

In addition to the case of multiple accreditation by the same State, Article 6 provides that two or more States may appoint the same

---

question. See Colliard, 'La Convention de Vienne sur les relations diplomatiques', *Annuaire français de droit international* (1961), p. 15.

[1] A proposal originally put forward by Italy (A/CONF.20/C.1/L.102) that the Convention should include a provision referring to the diplomatic corps failed of adoption, as it had during the discussions of the International Law Commission, chiefly on the ground that the corps, although it undoubtedly existed, had neither clearly defined functions nor independent legal standing.

[2] Article 17.

[3] Article 5, paragraph 1. If the head of mission is changed, the *agrément* of each of the receiving States is required. It may be noted that the British Ambassador to the Cameroons is accredited in addition to the Central African Republic, Chad and Gabon. Several other British Embassies in Africa also cover more than one country. *Diplomatic Service List, 1967.*

[4] Article 5, paragraph 3.

[5] The vote, taken in the plenary session, was 32 in favour, 27 against and 11 abstentions: *Official Records*, vol. I, p. 11. The Swiss representative referred to the preservation of the 'customary consultations'.

persons as head of mission unless objection is offered by the receiving State. This practice, which has always had some adherents, may well increase in coming years as regional movements develop in strength. The Scandinavian States have given serious consideration to the establishment of joint diplomatic missions, and Article 4(2) of the *Convention générale relative à la représentation diplomatique*, adopted in 1961 by members of the *Union africaine et malgache*, provides expressly for the appointment by Member States of common representatives to third countries.[1]

Other members of the staff

(*a*) *Appointment.* In the case of members of the staff, other than the head of mission (for whom the *agrément* of the receiving State must be obtained), the question of appointment is governed by Article 7, one of the most important, as well as one of the most obscure, clauses in the instrument. The Article states that, subject to the conditions contained in certain other provisions, the sending State 'may freely appoint the members of the staff of the mission'. An express exception is made in the case of service attachés, whose names the receiving State may require to be submitted beforehand for its approval.

The difficulty is to determine the precise scope and effect of the appointment made by the sending State, and, above all, the question whether appointment as such carries with it an obligation for the receiving State to accord the normal consequences, namely the grant of privileges and immunities. The principle involved was discussed at length by the International Law Commission at its ninth session in 1957, after Mr. Tunkin (USSR) had introduced a draft article which said simply,

The sending State may freely choose the other officials which it appoints to the mission.[2]

Mr. Verdross (Austria) proposed to add to this a further sentence:

Any State may, however, refuse to receive any person notified to it as having been appointed to a diplomatic mission.[3]

In his view the consent of the receiving State was required not only for the head of mission but also in respect of other members, the only

[1] Two or more States may send a joint special mission under Article 5 of the International Law Commission's proposals on special missions. *Report of the International Law Commission on the work of its nineteenth session, 1967, General Assembly Official Records, Twenty-second Session, Suppl. No 9* (A/6709/Rev.1).
[2] *Yearbook of the International Law Commission, 1957*, vol. I, p. 15.
[3] Ibid., p. 26.

difference lying in the form in which it was given. Whereas in the case
of an ambassador consent was given explicitly and in advance, in the
case of other members it might be given implicitly, either before entry
by the grant of an entry visa or by some act of acceptance performed
after arrival, such as inclusion in the diplomatic list. There is undoubtedly some practice in support of this approach. The Swiss
decision *In re Vitianu*[1] illustrates the contingency which is sought to
be guarded against. The defendant in that case entered Switzerland
as the representative of a Romanian commercial undertaking in
February 1947. In June 1948 the Romanian Legation told the Federal
Political Department that he had been appointed Economic Coun-
sellor. On 25 June the Department informed the Legation that no
decision had yet been taken regarding his acceptance. The Legation
was notified on 11 July that Vitianu's appointment was not acceptable;
on 13 July he was arrested and charged with an array of serious
offences ranging from the collection of political and economic intel-
ligence, to usury, bribery and malicious prosecution. The plea that
Vitianu enjoyed diplomatic immunity was rejected by the Federal
Tribunal, which held that no immunity need be accorded until the
receiving State had given its consent; it was not bound to accept the
person appointed merely by virtue of his nomination. The Tribunal
declared expressly that it was not sufficient to give the receiving State
the power to declare subsequently that the person was not accepted
and to request his recall, for this would enable the sending State to
free its own nationals (or, for that matter, those of other countries
also) from the jurisdiction of the receiving State, even though they
had been previously living in that country.

In the light of the conflicting proposals put forward, the International Law Commission was called upon to decide, in Mr. Tunkin's
words 'whether a person whom the sending State appointed to a
diplomatic mission—other than its head—was thenceforth regarded
ipso facto as a member of the mission, or whether he was not so regarded until the receiving State had given its consent even tacitly'.[2] A
number of members of the Commission declared that Mr. Verdross'
proposal did not represent the main prevailing practice and would, if
introduced, result in serious inconvenience to States. What would be
the position of a diplomatic agent who was told after he had entered

[1] *Annual Digest*, 1949, p. 281. Decisions on a partly similar basis were given in
B. v. M. and *United States ex rel. Roberto Santiesteban Casanova v. Fitzpatrick*,
although in these instances the plea was raised that the defendant was a member
of a mission to an international organization. See pp. 112 and 115 below.
[2] *Yearbook of the International Law Commission, 1957*, vol. I, p. 27.

the receiving State that his status was not recognized and that accordingly he did not enjoy privileges and immunities of any kind? Sufficient safeguard of the interests of the receiving State was provided, it was argued, by the fact that the receiving State could always refuse to grant an entry visa or declare the person not acceptable upon arrival. Mr. Verdross' proposal was finally rejected, by an extremely narrow margin,[1] and that of Mr. Tunkin accepted.[2] At the 1958 session of the Commission, the qualification was added that, in the case of military, naval or air attachés, the receiving State might require that their names be submitted for its prior approval.

The version approved by the International Law Commission was adopted by the Vienna Conference with only slight amendment.[3] An attempt was made, however, at the Conference to re-introduce in another guise the principle which Mr. Verdross had sought to invoke, namely, that the consent of the receiving State must have been obtained before that State can be called upon to acknowledge the consequences of an appointment. The French representative proposed an amendment distinguishing between appointment as such and the inclusion of the names of members of the diplomatic staff in the diplomatic list; entry on the list would constitute recognition of diplomatic status.[4] The arguments raised against this proposal were similar to those put forward in the International Law Commission. What would be the position of a diplomat between entry into the country and inclusion in the list? Furthermore the significance of the diplomatic list varied from country to country and in some instances had no particular legal value in court proceedings. Even if the receiving State refused to include someone in the list or to issue a diplomatic card, this would only mean, in the opinion of the representative of the USSR, that the State in question would be applying the *persona non grata* procedure[5]—i.e. the person affected would have to be treated as an already appointed diplomat. When, at the end of the discussion, the International Law Commission's draft was adopted, several speakers (in particular the delegate of Switzerland) indicated

---

[1] By nine votes to eight, with one abstention. Ibid., p. 29.

[2] By a majority of 14 votes to none with two abstentions. Ibid., p. 30. In its final form the action of the sending State was made subject to the draft articles relating to the appointment of non-nationals, the application of the *persona non grata* procedure, and the overall size of the mission.

[3] Appointments by the sending State were made subject also to the provisions of Article 5 relating to multiple assignment.

[4] A/CONF.20/C.1/L.1. And see the statement of the French representative, *Official Records*, vol. I, pp. 94–5.

[5] Ibid., p. 95.

nevertheless that, in the opinion of their Governments, the Article was to be interpreted as requiring the consent of the receiving State to any appointments, in accordance with prevailing custom.[1]

What then is the position finally arrived at? The situation may be summed up as follows: whereas in the case of the head of mission the advance consent of the receiving State must be obtained, or, in the case of service attachés, may be made a prior requirement if the receiving State so chooses, in all other cases the sending State is free to make appointments which are immediately effective. The exercise of the power of the sending State is subject, however, to the qualifications contained or implied in the text of the Convention or to the preservation of a contrary customary practice, such as that maintained by Switzerland. The limitations contained in the text relate to appointments to more than one State (Article 5, paragraph 1), the restrictions on appointment of non-nationals (Article 8) and on the size of the mission (Article 11), and, lastly, the safeguards of the *persona non grata* procedure (Article 9). Furthermore, although under the terms of Article 7 the sending State has a free choice in the matter of appointments in the sense that it is not obliged to submit names in advance, Article 10 requires that the receiving State must be notified of the appointment and arrival of members of the mission, as well as of their final departure or termination of functions.[2] In addition, the receiving State can make entry into the country dependent on the grant of an appropriate visa. The possibility accordingly exists for a member of the mission to be declared *non grata* or 'not acceptable', as expressly envisaged in Article 9, even before his actual arrival in the territory of the receiving State.

(b) *Appointment of non-nationals.* The receiving State is given special powers with respect to the appointment of persons who do not have the nationality of the sending State, in accordance with the premise that all members of the diplomatic staff should, in principle, be citizens of the State which appoints them.[3] The appointment of a national of the receiving State as a member of the diplomatic staff (including, conceivably, the head of mission himself) can only be made with the consent of the receiving State, which may be with-

---

[1] The interpretation of the Swiss representative, based on an Italian amendment (A/CONF.20/C.1/L.48), was supported by the delegate of Ireland; see also the statement of the French representative, *Official Records*, vol. I, pp. 97, 98.

[2] In the case of arrival and final departure prior notification must be given where possible: Article 10, paragraph 2.

[3] Article 8, paragraph 1.

drawn at any time.[1] The receiving State may reserve the same right in the case of nationals of a third State who are not also nationals of the sending State.[2]

No such condition is imposed with respect to the appointment of members of the mission staff who are of less than diplomatic rank since it was recognized that the work of the mission might well require the employment of subordinate personnel who have a knowledge of the language of the receiving State or of local conditions, or who perform routine tasks, for example, as typists, messengers and drivers.

Size of the mission and acceptance of particular categories of staff

Over the past twenty years not only has there been a large increase in the total number of missions sent between different countries (as there has in the number of States), there has also been a sharp rise in the number of personnel employed, at all levels, in individual missions. Although this has been justified by the greater range of activities undertaken it has presented receiving States with some awkward difficulties. If a single mission, even in a relatively minor State, may approach five hundred people or more, the problem of protection and of discreet surveillance may be considerable, not to mention the provision of housing, parking facilities, customs exemptions and the other accessories of diplomatic functions. There was general agreement, therefore, both in the International Law Commission and at the Vienna Conference, that some means should be found to limit the overall size of a mission. Under previously prevailing practice the sending State was at liberty to determine for itself how large its mission should be, the receiving State intervening only when it considered the number excessive; at that stage the matter was normally settled by negotiation. The principle that, where possible, the size of the mission should be fixed by mutual agreement, was retained, both in the International Law Commission's draft and in the Convention. In the absence of such agreement however, the receiving State is given power to require

that the size of a mission be kept within limits considered by it to be reasonable and normal, having regard to circumstances and conditions in the receiving State and to the needs of the particular mission.[3]

This formulation represented a significant change in two respects

[1] Article 8, paragraph 2. For the position as regards enjoyment of privileges and immunities by such persons see p. 78 below.   [2] Article 8, paragraph 3. Nepal made an express reservation under this provision when acceding to the Convention.   [3] Article 11, paragraph 1.

from that proposed by the Commission. Firstly, in place of the Commission's requirement that the receiving State might refuse to accept a size 'exceeding what is reasonable and normal', the Vienna Conference adopted an Argentine amendment[1] whereby it is for the receiving State to decide what it considers reasonable and normal. Secondly, the final version of the Convention does not make the settlement of disputes obligatory[2]—whereas, therefore, the International Law Commission's draft provided for an objective valuation ('what is reasonable and normal') in the absence of specific agreement, and, if a dispute arose, envisaged obligatory arbital or judicial settlement, the clause finally adopted increases the scope of the unilateral powers of the receiving State and reduces the arguments of the sending State to those of mere remonstrance if it considers that an abuse has occurred. As against this there is the consideration, which weighed with the Conference, that most States receive more mission staff than they send (the main exceptions being the major countries, which are also the ones which maintain the largest individual embassies). Faced with a situation in which the compulsory settlement of disputes was unlikely to be accepted, the Conference therefore adopted a justifiable choice in deciding that, subject to the qualifications specified, the final power of decision should rest with the receiving State.[3]

Besides the restrictions which it may impose on the size of the mission, the receiving State may refuse to accept officials of a particular category.[4] The conditions under which it may exercise this discretionary power are the same as those applicable in the case of limitations on size, with the addition that any refusal must be non-discriminatory, i.e. applied equally with respect to all States.[5] No such condition is imposed in the case of limitations on size, since it would be impossible to require that all the missions in a country should have the same number of staff.

[1] A/CONF.20/C.1/L.119.

[2] The International Law Commission's revised draft provided in Article 45 for the compulsory settlement of disputes. The provision concerned was replaced at the Vienna Conference by an Optional Protocol binding only on those States which accepted it; the Protocol entered into force on 24 April 1964; the States parties are listed on p. 129, n. 2, below.

[3] Four States, Byelorussia SSR, Mongolia, Ukrainian SSR and the USSR, have made reservations with respect to Article 11, paragraph 1, of the Convention; Canada, the Federal Republic of Germany, Luxembourg, Malta and the United Kingdom have registered their objections to some or all of these reservations, together with Tanzania (in respect of the USSR reservation).

[4] Article 11, paragraph 2.

[5] See p. 83 below.

TERMINATION OF FUNCTIONS OF MEMBERS OF THE STAFF

Modes of termination

Besides causes of a general nature which may lead to the termination of the functions of the members of the staff involved, such as the breaking off of diplomatic relations or the withdrawal of a mission, each State may take steps to bring the functions of individual staff members to an end. In the case of the sending State its powers are, in the last resort, those of an employer who can decide whether or not to retain personnel, and where they are to be deployed. Undoubtedly the commonest reason why the sending State may notify the receiving State that the functions of a diplomatic agent have ended is the decision of the sending State to transfer the agent concerned to another post.[1] The sending State may also choose to recall its envoy, as a step less than total breach of diplomatic relations, in the course of a political dispute—an action usually reciprocated by the receiving State. Other causes may be of a personal character, the retirement or death of the agent, for example, or his resignation from the service.

The receiving State is normally confined to the use of the *persona non grata* procedure if it wishes to end the functions of a particular diplomatic agent. Article 9 provides that, without being obliged to give reasons (although normally a State will do so, if only informally, in order to avoid the accusation of irresponsible behaviour), the receiving State may inform the sending State that a member of the diplomatic staff of a mission is no longer *persona grata* or, in the case of members of the staff in other categories, is 'not acceptable'.[2] In this event the sending State has a choice between recalling the person concerned[3] or terminating his functions (and notifying the receiving State accordingly). If the sending State declines to exercise this choice, or fails to do so within a reasonable period, the receiving State may notify the sending State that it refuses to recognize the individual as a member of the mission.[4] The reasons which may lead the receiving

---

[1] Article 43(*a*). The foreign ministry of the receiving State must be notified of the termination of the functions of all members of the mission under Article 10, paragraph 1(*a*) and (*d*).

[2] The variation in phraseology is based on usage and does not involve any difference of substance. The decision may be taken even before the person has arrived in the receiving State: Article 9, paragraph 1, *in fine*.

[3] Even in the case of nationals of the receiving State?

[4] Article 43(*b*). Another contingency expressly dealt with in the Convention is the withdrawal by the receiving State of its consent that one of its nationals be appointed to the diplomatic staff of a mission: Article 8, paragraph 2.

State to declare a member of the staff of a mission *persona non grata* or not acceptable are innumerable, the most frequent being a default in professional conduct (for example, interference in the internal affairs of the receiving State), or the commission of a serious crime or of a private act which reflects personal discredit on the man.

Facilitation of departure

It was agreed, with relatively little debate, that even in case of armed conflict the receiving State must grant facilities in order to enable persons enjoying privileges and immunities to leave at the earliest possible moment.[1] If necessary, means of transport are to be provided for such persons and their property. This requirement, which admits of an exception in the case of nationals of the receiving State and members of their families, has an evident functional justification.

FACILITATION OF THE WORK OF DIPLOMATIC MISSIONS

General facilities, including those relating to the use of premises

A mission operating in a foreign State has, *ex hypothesi*, no executive arm of its own which can place the mission directly in a position to fulfil its responsibilities. In carrying out its functions the mission is dependent on the host Government, which is therefore under an obligation to facilitate the active performance of the mission's tasks, as well as being under a duty to provide an adequate degree of protection and immunity. Besides granting freedom of movement to members of the staff of the mission and allowing the mission itself to enjoy free communication, the receiving State is specifically required to accord 'full facilities' for the execution of the functions of the mission.[2] As the International Law Commission pointed out in its commentary, a diplomatic mission may often need assistance at the time of its installation;[3] when the local authorities control the issue of building permits, for example, or act as the supplier of telephones and other services, their co-operation may be essential to avoid long delays. The Commission also drew attention to the fact that the mission may require the help of the receiving State in performing its immediate functions, in particular as regards the collection of information on local conditions. A proposal that missions should, amongst the facilities afforded them, receive the benefits of the most favourable exchange rate, was not accepted, however, in part owing

[1] Article 44.   [2] Article 25.
[3] *Yearbook of the International Law Commission, 1958*, vol. II, p. 96.

to the difficulty of showing why the receiving State should be under an obligation to grant *the* most favourable rate (as opposed to *a* favourable rate) and in part owing to the complicated nature of the subject-matter.[1]

The only facility dealt with specifically in the text of the Convention concerns the acquisition or obtaining of premises. Article 21 provides, in carefully chosen language, that the receiving State shall 'either facilitate the acquisition on its territory, in accordance with its laws, by the sending State of premises necessary for its mission or assist the latter in obtaining accommodation in some other way'. Under the second paragraph of the Article the receiving State is required 'where necessary' to assist missions to obtain suitable accommodation for their staff.[2] In the course of its legislative history this provision underwent a distinct if subtle modification. As originally proposed, it was intended to establish the right of the sending State to obtain mission premises in countries which placed restrictions on the alienation of land, either with respect to foreigners in general or to foreign Governments in particular, or where the land was owned exclusively by the State.[3] The draft article prepared by the International Law Commission[4] did not require the receiving State to do more than permit the sending State to acquire property; if the receiving State declined to do so, however, it was then obliged to ensure that adequate accommodation was made available. At the Vienna Convention the article was changed so as to weaken but, at the same time, to widen the obligation. Instead of being required to 'permit' the acquisition of premises, the receiving State must either 'facilitate' their acquisition, 'in accordance with its laws', or 'assist' the sending State in obtaining accommodation in some other way. Thus, on the one hand, a receiving State which in principle allows the acquisition of property by foreign Governments is also obliged to facilitate such acquisition and, on the other, receiving States which do not allow such acquisition cannot rely (it is submitted) on the phrase referring to local law in order to defeat the object of the Article. Although for present purposes this interpretation must suffice it is

---

[1] *Yearbook of the International Law Commission, 1958*, vol. I, pp. 136–7.

[2] Although Article 21, paragraph 1, is in any case cast in terms wide enough to include the accommodation of the head of mission, the definition of the 'premises of the mission' given in Article 1(*i*) includes the residence of the head of mission— i.e. the acquisition of his residence falls under paragraph 1, not paragraph 2, of Article 21.

[3] See *Yearbook of the International Law Commission, 1957*, vol. I, pp. 60–2.

[4] Article 19, *Yearbook of the International Law Commission, 1958*, vol. II, p. 95.

doubtful if the foreign offices of the world have concluded their discussion of the precise scope of this provision.

Once acquired—which has begun to seem a somewhat difficult process—the premises may be used for the purposes of the mission, though not for any other,[1] as determined by the sending State. That State may not, however, set up subsidiary offices away from the main location of the mission, which is normally established at the seat of the Government,[2] without the consent of the receiving State. This provision[3] was introduced at the suggestion of the Netherlands Government which objected to the tendency of foreign Governments to transfer parts of their diplomatic missions away from The Hague to Amsterdam or Rotterdam. A number of other countries face similar problems.[4] Whilst the possibility, envisaged by both the Diplomatic and Consular Conventions, of the performance of consular functions by diplomatic missions, makes the issue a real one for all States, the fact that the Diplomatic Convention envisages a 'divided' mission, with offices scattered across the country, may be of particular advantage to States seeking to observe local conditions and to secure prompt access to their nationals in all parts of the receiving State.

Freedom of movement

One of the facilities required for performance of a mission's functions is that its members should enjoy freedom of movement and travel. As was said in the International Law Commission, and as subsequent commentators have repeated, it would not have been considered necessary in a former age to include a provision designed to safeguard this freedom.[5] Although some restrictions on security grounds have always been acknowledged, for example as regards fortified or frontier zones, only in the past twenty years has the exception come to dwarf the general principle that, in order to fulfil the functions of observing local conditions, protecting nationals and repre-

[1] Article 41, paragraph 3.
[2] But not invariably, e.g., in Israel, where the transfer of the seat of Government from Tel Aviv to Jerusalem in 1953 resulted in diplomatic protests and the refusal of a number of States to move their embassies.
[3] Article 12. For the views of the Netherlands see the statement of Mr. François, *Yearbook of the International Law Commission, 1958*, vol. I, p. 113.
[4] Some of the other cases mentioned were Germany (Bonn, Cologne and Frankfurt), Switzerland (Berne and Geneva), and the United States (Washington and New York).
[5] See *Yearbook of the International Law Commission, 1957*, vol. I, pp. 85–7, especially the remarks of Sir Gerald Fitzmaurice (United Kingdom).

senting the sending State throughout the country, the members of the mission should enjoy a general freedom of movement in the territory of the receiving State. Whatever the ultimate justification, or lack of it, the practice has grown for first one receiving State, and then the other on grounds of reciprocity, to introduce restrictions on the movements of the diplomats accredited to it. Such restrictions, which have mostly been applied in the case of Western diplomats stationed in Eastern Europe and vice versa, as part of the general East–West tension,[1] have made journeys beyond a given radius of the capital[2] dependent on notification to the authorities of the host State, which have then decided whether or not the journey might be made and under what conditions (e.g. only in a chauffeur-driven car, supplied by the host State, and along a prescribed route). The time-honoured maxim *ne impediatur legatio* has in this way been deprived of much of its literal meaning.

The clause adopted by the Vienna Conference represents an attempt to turn the tide.[3] Whilst acknowledging that restrictions may be imposed for reasons of national security, the thrust of the Article, as was made clear during the debates, is to emphasize that the receiving State is not at liberty to render the principle of freedom of movement illusory—that, in short, the exceptions are to remain limited exceptions. States are, of course, prone to keep a watchful eye on each other's diplomats—a perennial tendency but one which has reached excessive proportions in recent years. It is to be hoped that the signs of greater mutual confidence which the Vienna Convention itself represents will help to produce an improvement as regards at least a greater freedom of movement and travel. Even where the States concerned are both parties to the Convention, however, the exception which is allowed, on grounds of reciprocity, to the principle of non-discrimination renders the Convention alone an incomplete remedy—an improvement in the machinery for the conduct of diplomatic relations cannot, though it may help, substitute for an improvement in the content of those relations themselves.

[1] Though not exclusively, see the USSR note to China, 9 February 1967.
[2] Approximately 40 km. in the case of Moscow in 1953, Perrenoud, 'Les restrictions à la liberté de déplacement des diplomates', *Revue générale de droit international public* (1953), p. 444; 25 miles in the case of New York or Washington, *Department of State Bulletin*, 49 (1963), pp. 855, 860; and 35 miles in the case of London, *British Practice in International Law, 1963–I*, ed. Lauterpacht, p. 32, quoting the reply of the Lord Privy Seal in the House of Commons. The United Kingdom presently applies restrictions only with respect to USSR and Chinese mission staff and has frequently declared its willingness to abolish all restrictions on a reciprocal basis.   [3] Article 26.

Freedom of communication

An individual mission performs its task as a component part of a network; on the one hand it collects and relays information and, on the other, it receives messages, either from the foreign ministry, which from the centre directs the whole, or from other offices of the sending State. Unless the mission enjoyed security in the sending and receiving of information its work would be severely hampered—it would not be possible to send a frank report on local conditions or on the progress of negotiations if the receiving State could look over the mission's shoulder. The need that the mission should enjoy freedom of communication in this respect has always been recognized, if not invariably respected.[1] The opening words of Article 27 prescribe the general principle involved: 'The receiving State shall permit and protect free communication on the part of the mission for all official purposes.' This expression of the twofold nature of the obligation of the receiving State—to allow the mission to enjoy free communication, and to ensure the inviolability of the means used—remains in the classic pattern. The Vienna Conference, like the International Law Commission before it, found it necessary, however, to re-assess the extent of this obligation, and of the freedom accorded to the mission, in the light of changed methods of communication, most notably as regards the use of air transport and of wireless transmitters. The result, as set out in the detailed provisions of Article 27, constitutes in most (but not all) instances an extension, as well as a consolidation, of the rights previously enjoyed by diplomatic missions.

Thus the scope of the 'official purposes' for which missions are granted an unhindered right of communication includes not only communications with the Government of the sending State and consular offices in the receiving State (which had always been allowed), but also those with authorities of the sending State situated in third States, with nationals of the sending State, with missions and consulates of other Governments, and with international organizations.[2] In messages with the home Government and its offices elsewhere, wherever situated, the mission may employ 'all appropriate means',

[1] The waylaying of couriers, the use of bribes and the deciphering of codes was a standard sixteenth- and seventeenth-century practice. In a *tour de force* of such endeavours Gondomar, the Spanish Ambassador to James I, regularly obtained information of discussions in the royal council, only to have his own dispatches reported back to the King by the English Ambassador to Madrid. Despite this, the Spanish Ambassador was considered an outstanding success at his post. For the full story see Mattingly, *Renaissance Diplomacy* (1955), pp. 260-1.

[2] *Yearbook of the International Law Commission, 1958*, vol. II, p. 97.

including the use of diplomatic couriers and other direct, confidential modes of communication. Traditionally a mission enjoyed an unfettered discretion in the choice of means only with respect to communications exchanged with its Government and with consulates under its authority situated in the receiving State; items of correspondence to and from missions in third States had to be sent via the sending State or were transmitted by the foreign ministry of the receiving State—in either event a lengthy and expensive process. The reference to 'all appropriate means' permits the employment of all the means now available—post, telephone, telegraph, diplomatic bag or courier, and the use of codes or ciphers. Only in the case of wireless transmitters is a limitation placed upon the freedom of the sending State to determine how its official communications shall be sent; the installation and use of a wireless transmitter within the premises of a mission is made dependent on the consent of the receiving State.

This issue caused extensive debate during the preparation of the Convention, as the legal and practical factors were paraded. As was said in the International Law Commission, the use of 'diplomatic wireless' is now quasi-universal and has virtually superseded other means of transmitting messages,[1] at least amongst States which have the resources and skilled personnel necessary for its maintenance. By means of a powerful transmitter in the sending State, aided by relay stations,[2] radio messages can be passed virtually simultaneously to embassies in other States, and the replies sent back again. The transmitters, which use code or cipher for confidential messages, are not suitable for voice transmission, and thus can not be used for purposes of propaganda or direct intervention over local broadcasting systems.[3] Furthermore, once installed, the cost of sending messages by this means is much cheaper than by the use of commercial radio or telegraph.[4] Nevertheless the employment of wireless transmitters, as a matter of right, encountered profound opposition amongst

---

[1] Sir Gerald Fitzmaurice, *Yearbook of the International Law Commission, 1957*, vol. I, p. 76.

[2] The United Kingdom is now considering the use of a communications satellite. It is said that, with the new methods of transmission 'such as pulsed code modulation and spectrum spread' available by this type of radio link, messages can be sent in codes that are almost impossible to crack; satellites are vulnerable to jamming however. *The Times*, 2 February 1967, p. 12, col. 3—appropriately enough reported by 'Our Science Reporter'.

[3] As was emphasized by the United Kingdom representative at the Vienna Conference, *Official Records*, vol. I, p. 177.

[4] Delegate of Israel, ibid., vol. I, p. 158.

States not presently enjoying such means.[1] Various arguments were advanced against the unrestricted installation and use of wireless transmitters. From a jurisprudential standpoint it was said that, since the Conference had rejected the theory of exterritoriality, sending States could not automatically claim to use their premises as they wished, in disregard of local law. If forty or more States were to go on the air it would in any case be necessary, if only for practical reasons, to regulate the distribution of frequencies. The relationship between the Vienna Convention and existing telecommunication agreements was also mentioned.[2] In addition, the needs of national security weighed heavily in determining the attitude of many developing countries.[3] Whereas the principle of freedom of movement was seen primarily against the background of East–West conflict, the question of the free employment of wireless transmitters effectively ranged North against South, and the deployment of the diplomatic skills of the developed States,[4] did not produce any major shift in attitude. It is difficult not to sympathize with both groups. On the one hand, 'diplomatic wireless' offers an unequalled means for the swift exchange of messages and it is on the States now possessing such means that, for better or worse, the peace of the world chiefly depends; on the other hand, it is a disturbing thought for Governments which do not enjoy these facilities that the ambassadors of the major powers may be more speedily informed about activities, including possibly activities taking place in the host State, than the authorities of the host State themselves. In the event it was finally agreed that the consent of the receiving State should be required both for the installation and for the use of a wireless transmitter by a diplomatic mission.[5]

[1] Kerley gives a detailed legislative history, 'Some Aspects of the Vienna Conference on Diplomatic Intercourse and Immunities'. *American Journal of International Law*, 56 (1962), pp. 111–16.

[2] A matter on which different opinions were expressed, as they were on the question of the extent of the obligations (if any) imposed under existing telecommunications conventions and regulations. It is undeniable that diplomatic messages sent by cable are granted priority in times of emergency—and that national legislation may suspend diplomatic transmissions in the event of a national crisis; see the *Décret* No. 52–1404 cited in Kiss, *Répertoire de la pratique française en matière de droit international public* (1965), tome III, no. 642, p. 359.

[3] Delegate of Nigeria, *Official Records*, vol. I, p. 178.

[4] Including, on this issue, USSR and the United States, as well as France, Germany and the United Kingdom. Note the United Kingdom amendment (A/CONF.20/C.1/L.291) introduced after an adjournment and informal negotiations, in an effort to reach agreement.

[5] Article 27, paragraph 1.

The remaining provisions relating to communications caused less debate. 'Official correspondence', defined as including 'all correspondence relating to the mission and its functions',[1] is declared inviolable. The limits of this obligation are made more specific in the case of the diplomatic bag, which may not be 'opened or detained'.[2] There were numerous references during the discussions to the scrutiny, not amounting to opening or detaining the bag, which customs and other officials might make of the bag. The use of X-ray machines, geiger counters, and the like was not decried as an infringement of inviolability; international law does not apparently include the notion of constructive entry. Nevertheless, all attempts to give the receiving State power to open the bag were unsuccessful—even with the consent of the foreign ministry if grave abuse was suspected, and in the presence of a representative of the mission.[3] The right to reject the bag, if the mission declined to open it, was also turned down. The principle thus stands more absolute than ever. Faced with a choice between possible abuse by the receiving State (which would presumably be officially motivated) or by the sending State (which might be for private rather than for official purposes), States considered the latter contingency less detrimental to their interests. It was emphasized that sending States were under a duty not to abuse the rights accorded to them with respect to the diplomatic bag—but the task of ensuring observation of that duty was not entrusted to the receiving State. Furthermore, as was pointed out by the USSR delegate,[4] although the diplomatic bag may contain only 'diplomatic documents or articles intended for official use',[5] the International Law Commission avoided the interpretation that the bag is inviolable only so long as it included official articles—inviolability is not conditional on observance of correct usage; the point is indicative of the extreme importance which States attach to the principle that the diplomatic bag should in no circumstances be subject to restraint.

The diplomatic bag, which may constitute a number of packages bearing 'visible external marks of their character'[6] may be sent

---

[1] Article 27, paragraph 2. [2] Article 27, paragraph 3.

[3] A/CONF.20/C.1/L.125, proposed by France.

[4] *Official Records*, vol. I, p. 179.

[5] Article 27, paragraph 4. Far from being a few letters, the amount moved by diplomatic bag may be considerable indeed. Mr. Bartoš (Yugoslavia) referred to embassies in Belgrade receiving 300–500 kilograms of 'diplomatic mail' per consignment and reaching a total of some 50 tons a year. *Yearbook of the International Law Commission, 1957*, vol. I, p. 77.

[6] Article 27, paragraph 4.

either unaccompanied or entrusted to a diplomatic courier provided with an official document (usually a diplomatic passport) indicating his status and the number of packages he is accompanying.[1] The receiving State, and any transit State,[2] is obliged to protect the courier in the exercise of his functions; in particular he enjoys personal inviolability and may not be arrested or detained. Where an *ad hoc* diplomatic courier is designated, these immunities cease when the courier has delivered the bag to its consignee.[3] Provision is also made for the case where the diplomatic bag is entrusted to the captain of a commercial aircraft, an increasingly common practice. Although the captain is given an official document listing the number of packages, he is not considered a diplomatic courier; the matter is different where the pilot is flying a plane used solely for the purposes of transporting diplomatic mail and members of diplomatic missions.[4]

[1] Article 27, paragraph 5.
[2] Article 40, paragraphs 3 and 4. See pp. 88–9 below.
[3] Article 27, paragraph 6.
[4] *Yearbook of the International Law Commission, 1958*, vol. II, p. 97.

Chapter III

INVIOLABILITY AND JURISDICTIONAL IMMUNITY

INVIOLABILITY

THE receiving State is under a duty to ensure that the mission is not subject to constraint, and is indeed actively protected, in the exercise of the means available to it for the performance of its tasks. An assured inviolability and security must therefore be provided both in respect of the use of premises and other forms of property (furnishings, means of transport, documents and correspondence) and as regards the personnel of the mission. This obligation stands half-way between the provision of assistance by the receiving State (as, for example, in the case of obtaining premises and accommodation) and the recognition of exceptions from local law and jurisdiction —the province of immunities proper. Since the limitations imposed may fall into more than one category, the dividing line between these various categories cannot be drawn with precision. Nevertheless the sphere of inviolability has two characteristics which serve to distinguish it: firstly, the receiving State must ensure that its own agents do not infringe the inviolability of the mission, and, secondly, it is under a duty to protect the mission against acts of interference by private persons.

Inviolability of premises

The mission is granted inviolability in respect of its premises so that it may enjoy the *franchise de l'hôtel*, that is to say the use of premises for the purposes of the mission's functions, in the manner chosen by the sending State.[1] Historically the grant of the *franchise* probably owes its origin to the assertion during the seventeenth century of the right of the envoy and his suite to worship according to the rites of their sovereign; *cuius regis eius religio*.[2] In view of the difficulties

---

[1] There was, in the days before organized police forces, a *franchise de quartier*, a general freedom from the operation of the law for all living within the shelter of the ambassador's residence—but this has long ago died out.

[2] See Mattingly, *Renaissance Diplomacy* (1955), p. 280.

41

experienced in establishing this *droit de chapelle*, there is some irony in noting that neither the International Law Commission nor the Vienna Conference found it necessary to include a provision on the subject; indeed, at the Conference not a single reference was made to it. During the discussions of the International Law Commission in 1957 the conclusion was reached that the principle was now self-evident, the only qualification being that the chapel should be situated within mission premises and not made open to the general public.[1] The Conference did, however, decide, in view of the restrictions placed by certain countries on the use of foreign insignia to mention expressly the right of the mission to display the flag and emblem of the sending State.[2] Whilst there was some support at the Conference for making this entitlement subject to the laws of the receiving State, no express amendment was pressed on the ground that exercise of the right was in any case subject to the provisions of Article 41, specifying the obligation of persons enjoying privileges and immunities to respect the laws and regulations of the receiving State. Although the sending State is therefore at liberty to show its flag and emblem, the receiving State is given some safeguard in the event that, for example in time of national emergency, it becomes necessary to regulate their display.

The discretion of the sending State with regard to the occupation of mission premises is subject only to the broad qualification contained in paragraph 3 of Article 41, which declares that such premises must not be used 'in any manner incompatible with the functions of the mission', as prescribed in Article 3 of the Convention, or 'by other rules of general international law or by any special agreements in force between the sending and receiving State'. Within these limits, which deny the sending State the right to employ its premises as, for example, a public school or library, unless agreement has been given, or for the purposes of conducting espionage activities,[3] the sending State is free to determine for itself how its premises shall be used. The reference in Article 41 to 'special agreements' is intended to permit, *inter alia*, the use of mission premises for providing diplo-

---

[1] *Yearbook of the International Law Commission, 1957*, vol. I, pp. 70–1.

[2] Article 20. Although not mentioned, in accordance with international usage members of the mission may perform the national anthem; this may not be done in public, however, unlike the case of the flag and emblem, the object of which is public display. Kiss, *Répertoire de la pratique française en matière de droit international public* (1965), tome III, no. 615, p. 347.

[3] Could a receiving State, on grounds of self-defence, authorize a friendly State to conduct espionage (or counter-espionage) activities from its embassy, directed against infiltrators from a third State, or against disaffected nationals?

matic asylum where the two States have accepted this practice.[1] The International Law Commission did not otherwise touch on the question of diplomatic asylum, nor were any formal amendments on this topic introduced at the Vienna Conference. Although, as was said during the discussion, the issue of diplomatic asylum was more suitable for consideration as part of the general problem of asylum, the Commission and the Conference were, in practical terms, bound by the decision of the Sixth Committee in 1952, rejecting a Colombian proposal that asylum should be included amongst the diplomatic topics to be examined by the International Law Commission.[2] In view of the continued importance of the question, not only in Latin America but elsewhere, the omission of an express provision is to be regretted, even though the issue involved is one on which States were unlikely to reach easy agreement.

As regards the definition of the premises for which inviolability may be claimed, the Vienna Convention makes provision both for the premises of the mission itself, in the sense of the mission buildings and appurtenant land,[3] and for the private residences of members of the diplomatic[4] and administrative staff.[5] The only difference in the two cases is that whereas the inviolability, and the immunity, of the premises of the mission is a distinct 'form of State immunity attaching to a building used for government purposes',[6] the inviolability of the residence remains a consequence of the diplomatic status of the occupant. The degree of inviolability to be afforded is the same in each instance. It makes no difference that the premises are not owned outright by the sending State or by the individual member of the staff—in the case of premises the only interest required is that of *de facto* occupancy and use; in this context the theory of 'function' has been followed, and not the more extreme versions of 'exterritoriality'.[7]

[1] Mr. Padilla Nervo (Mexico), *Yearbook of the International Law Commission 1957*, vol. I, p. 144.

[2] See, Report of the Committee of the Whole, paragraph 105, *Official Records*, vol. II, p. 57, and Raton, 'Travaux de la Commission juridique de l'Assemblée Générale des Nations Unies', *Annuaire français de droit international* (1959), pp. 470–2.

[3] Article 22, paragraph 1, and Article 1(*i*).

[4] Article 30, paragraph 1. Such premises may be temporary, e.g. hotel rooms.

[5] Article 37, paragraph 2.

[6] Sir Gerald Fitzmaurice, *Yearbook of the International Law Commission, 1957*, vol. I, p. 53.

[7] See Romberg, 'The Immunity of Embassy Premises', *British Year Book of International Law*, XXXV (1959), p. 235, for an account of four cases which were decided on this basis, following extensive review, and *Petrocchino v. Swedish State*,

Turning to the responsibilities of the receiving State, it is obliged, firstly, to ensure that its agents do not enter the premises of the mission or those used by the two categories of staff mentioned above, except with the consent of the head of the mission. After long discussion the International Law Commission decided that no exceptions should be made to this rule,[1] even in the event of emergency, a decision upheld at the Conference. It was argued, on the one hand, that it would be a manifest abuse, and indeed an instance of outright foolishness, if, in the event of a fire threatening the neighbourhood, or of a man shooting with a rifle from the windows of a mission, the local authorities were not able to go in and deal with the matter. The advocates of this view received support from those whose concern was with the right of eminent domain—the expropriation of land for public purposes, such as road widening and other acts of town planning. Neither set of arguments was accepted however; in this instance, as in others, the Conference felt that, so far as the express admission of exceptions was concerned, *définir, c'est finir*. If a unilateral power of determination were given to the receiving State in one context, for example, with respect to the outbreak of fire, by parity of reasoning the power should extend, or might in practice be extended, to acts based on other paramount necessities, such as those of state security—and this no sending State wished to see. Thus, even if a mission fails to use its premises in accordance with legitimate purposes, its inviolability must still be respected by the receiving State.[2] As is made clear, *ex abundante cautela*, in Article 22, paragraph 3, it makes no difference that judicial or similar authorization has been given, directed against the mission premises or the property thereon; the authorities of the receiving State may not enter, even in pursuance of official instructions, in order to search or requisition

---

Annual Digest, 1929–30, p. 306, which, though in terms referring to exterritoriality, made the actual application of this theory dependent on the requirements of functional use.

[1] Nor even referred to in the commentary. *Yearbook of the International Law Commission, 1958*, vol. II, p. 130.

[2] In the celebrated case of Sun Yat Sen, who was held prisoner in the Chinese Legation in London in 1896, the British authorities refrained from the direct use of force to secure his release and relied on diplomatic protest. See McNair, *International Law Opinions* (1956), vol. I, p. 85. N.B. An application for habeas corpus was refused, op. cit., p. 88. On one occasion the French judicial police entered the USSR Embassy in Paris in order to protect the family of a member of the Embassy who had fled; it was alleged that the family were being kept prisoner and were in danger of being executed. Kiss, op. cit., no. 636, p. 357.

the premises or in order to execute an order of attachment or execution.

The same rule applies with respect to the issue, or attempted issue, of writs within diplomatic premises. A corollary of the immunity from jurisdiction normally enjoyed by members of mission staff, the mere service of process has traditionally been regarded as in itself an affront to the dignity and respect due to the mission, and therefore forbidden even where the writ was served without crossing the threshold—as where the process server lay in wait at the door. This still leaves open the possibility, in which there has been some variation in practice, that the writ or other judicial notice might be served through the post or transmitted by the ministry for foreign affairs. Having regard to the differences in the procedures available in various countries—whereas some normally insist on personal service others allow service by post or similar methods—the International Law Commission decided in its commentary at least not to forbid the possible use of means which did not involve physical violation of the premises.[1] At the Vienna Conference, however, an amendment introduced by Japan, designed to obtain a definite ruling one way or the other, was withdrawn 'on the understanding that it was the unanimous interpretation of the Committee that no writ could be served, even by post, within the premises of a diplomatic mission'.[2] On this

[1] *Yearbook of the International Law Commission, 1958*, vol. II, p. 95.
[2] *Official Records*, vol. I, p. 141. That this was the unanimous interpretation of the Committee of the Whole does not clearly emerge from the written records. The actual terms of the Japanese amendment ('No writ may be served by a process server within the premises of the Mission': A/CONF/C.1/L.146) went beyond the mere service of process by post, but the comments, both written and oral, of the Japanese Government made it clear that it was the possibility of service by post that was aimed at. Only seven speakers, apart from the Japanese representative himself, referred to the amendment: one (Argentina) was against the proposal and one (Ghana) supported it; two (Spain and France) considered that the matter would be dealt with more appropriately under the provision relating to the conduct of official business through the ministry of foreign affairs of the receiving State; Turkey also considered that a writ could be transmitted through the foreign ministry—or by post; the USSR, though not opposed to the amendment, considered that the existing text would cover the case—and therefore proposed to vote against the amendment. This was also apparently the view of Norway. These remarks, together with those of the majority of other speakers who indicated that they were not prepared to accept changes in the original draft article, support the view expressed by the United Kingdom delegate that the various amendments proposed (including the Japanese proposal) would not in fact have been accepted if put to the vote. Since it was the opinion of the Japanese Government that, without its amendment, the draft article prepared by the International Law Commission did not make it self-evident that service by post was allowed, the Japanese representative withdrew his amendment on the negative understanding quoted in the text. No delegate subsequently objected to his statement, which

basis the sole channel for the service of process is through the ministry for foreign affairs. Such ministries are not, however, usually eager to transmit a summons or to serve process on a diplomatic representative, unless they have learnt by discreet inquiry beforehand that the embassy or person concerned is prepared to accept the document.[1]

The second aspect of the responsibility of the receiving State is its obligation to provide protection for the premises of the mission. As is said in the Convention, the receiving State is under a 'special duty'—that is to say, one over and above that owed to preserve law and order generally and to safeguard the homes of foreigners—'to take all appropriate steps to protect the premises of the mission against any intrusion or damage and to prevent any disturbance of the peace of the mission or impairment of its dignity'.[2] The need for this provision hardly requires argument—apart from the general principle involved, newspapers have made their readers fully familiar with reports that an embassy building has been attacked, as the culminating point of a well-organized demonstration; in some cases the police battle with the demonstrators, in others they are alleged to stand passively by. Demonstrations against foreign Governments and their premises, usually the product of East–West or anti-colonialist tensions,[3] do not in themselves give rise to international responsi-

---

was in clear terms and included in the records at the express request of the Japanese speaker.

[1] See the detailed reply of the United States Department of State to the Justice Department, *American Journal of International Law*, 59 (1965), pp. 110–11. There is no reason to suppose that the attitude of the State Department is not that of other foreign ministries; see, for example, the remarks of Sir Gerald Fitzmaurice, *Yearbook of the International Law Commission, 1958*, vol. II, p. 131, at paragraph 36.

[2] Article 22, paragraph 2.

[3] See the long catalogue in Dehaussy, 'De l'inviolabilité des hôtels diplomatiques', *Journal du droit international*, 1956, p. 596. More recent cases include the sack of the British Embassy in Djakarta in 1963. After attempts had been made to enter the strongroom the British Ambassador returned, accompanied by members of the diplomatic corps, and succeeded in re-establishing control; the archives were then destroyed under supervision: *British Practice in International Law 1963—II*, p. 133. In September 1966 the Portuguese Embassy in Kinshasha was wrecked and members of the staff removed. The Congolese Prime Minister and Foreign Minister went in person to the scene the next day, when a further demonstration took place, to persuade the crowd to disperse. This incident, which occurred during Security Council discussion of a Congolese complaint of Portuguese intervention, was reported to the United Nations (see document S/7506, dated 26 September 1966, and records of 1302nd and 1304th meetings of the Security Council, 30 September and 13 October 1966). The growing practice of informing the United Nations of serious breaches of diplomatic law is justified

bility unless the receiving State has failed to take the necessary action to limit the attack or punish the offenders. Where the receiving State has advance notice, whether from the mission itself or as a matter of public knowledge, it can order its police to control the outbreak; in a number of capitals local ordinances forbid demonstrations and acts of picketing directed against foreign missions.[1]

If a disturbance does take place, affecting the work of the mission, the local authorities will be required to put an end to it, without waiting to be called upon to do so by the mission. They may not, however, enter the premises of the mission, even if an intrusion occurs, unless the head of the mission gives his consent; if requested to remove intruders, they must nevertheless proceed with all reasonable dispatch. In such circumstances the duty of the receiving State is not merely that of providing external protection but of restoring the mission to its former situation in the hands of the mission staff. This aspect of the obligation imposed on the receiving State came to the fore in the unusual circumstances of what is known as the 'Romanian Legation in Berne' case.[2] In 1955, during the night of 14–15 February, a group of Romanian emigrés who had crossed the border from Germany gained possession of the Romanian Legation in Berne. They shot a chauffeur, who later died, and took prisoner the other members of the Legation staff. The Legation was surrounded by heavily armed police from three o'clock on. By 7.30 a.m. a meeting of the Swiss Federal Council had been held, when it was decided, upon the advice of the head of the Berne police, that no immediate attempt should be made to re-take the premises, despite the request of the available Romanian official that this should be done. The intruders, who released their prisoners at 7.15 a.m., were thought to be well

---

by the attention which the complaint receives, in a milieu of professional diplomats, and by the threat to international peace and stability which such attacks represent.

The USSR note to China of 9 February 1967 complained that the demonstrations and other activities directed against the Soviet Embassy in Peking were effectively preventing the Mission from performing its functions.

[1] E.g. the Joint Resolution approved by the United States Congress on 15 February 1938. Stowell, *American Journal of International Law*, 32 (1938), p. 344. The United States authorities have declined to adopt similar measures in New York.

[2] See Dehaussy, loc. cit., *Journal du droit international* (1956), p. 596, Louis-Lucas, 'L'affaire de la Légation de Roumanie à Berne', *Annuaire français de droit international* (1955), p. 175, and Perrin, 'L'agression contre la Légation de Roumanie à Berne et le fondément de la responsabilité internationale dans les délits d'omission', *Revue générale de droit international public*, XXVIII–LXI (1957), p. 410.

supplied with arms. There the matter stood until the intruders finally surrendered at 4.30 p.m. on 16 February, in response to a promise which they had given earlier. In diplomatic notes the Romanian Government complained that the Swiss Government had not prevented the attack, that it should have acted more promptly and vigorously in expelling the intruders, and that the wrongdoers should be handed over to Romania for punishment. As regards the first two arguments, the answer lies in the assessment, in the light of the particular facts, of the adequacy of the steps taken.[1] As regards the punishment of wrongdoers, it is submitted that the attitude of Switzerland, in declining to surrender the offenders to Romania, is in accordance with established doctrine and practice. Crimes under local law committed on mission premises by persons not themselves enjoying immunity do not for that reason escape the jurisdiction of the courts of the receiving State. Even when greater weight was attached to the notion of exterritoriality of mission premises than is presently the case, it was held that persons committing crimes within embassy premises were punishable under the ordinary law of the land.[2] Indeed, following attacks on the premises and personnel of a mission, the receiving State is under a duty to pursue the offenders and to ensure that proceedings are taken against them.

Inviolability of property

'Property' is used here in a wider sense than that used in the text of the Convention, where it is employed as a residual term, after individual forms of property have been singled out for special mention. In effect, by reason of their importance certain forms of property are accorded inviolability in their own right, whilst other forms

[1] See Dehaussy, Louis-Lucas and Perrin, idem., for the pros and cons which can be advanced; the arguments of the last-named, based on a more complete account of the facts, are to be preferred as regards at least the particular incident.
[2] The leading precedent is the *Afghan Embassy Case, Annual Digest*, 1933–4, p. 385, where the *Reichsgericht* upheld the jurisdiction of the German courts to try the murderer of the Afghan Minister to Berlin. The more difficult cases are: (*i*) where the author of the act is himself protected by immunity (see the case of the fatal wounding of a member of the Dominican Embassy in the Dominican Consulate in London, mentioned by Lyons, 'Diplomatic Immunities—Some Minor Points', *British Year Book of International Law*, xxxiv (1958), p. 368, at p. 373); (*ii*) where it is not possible under local law to pursue the action effectively unless the diplomat concerned in the case is willing to appear in court and, if necessary, to submit to cross-examination; and (*iii*), where the offence is cognizable by the law of the sending State but not by that of the receiving State (e.g. a false statement to an embassy official; see Moore, *Digest of International Law* (1906), vol. ii, pp. 266–7).

receive protection indirectly, usually in consequence of the inviolability of the premises in which they are situated.

(a) *Archives and documents.* In order to preserve them from being seen by unauthorized eyes and, in particular, from being requested for production in judicial proceedings, mission archives and documents are declared inviolable. At the Vienna Conference, the words 'at any time and wherever they may be' were specially added to the future Article 24 so as to remove any doubt that the inviolability of these items is independent of that of the persons to whom they may be entrusted or of the premises where they are normally to be found. This clear language, which is based on a similar provision in the Convention on the Privileges and Immunities of the United Nations,[1] does not make it altogether obvious what happens if the mission itself, or members of its personnel, fail to take proper care of the documents so that they fall into the wrong hands. Is the receiving State still obliged to treat them as inviolable? What, in any case, can inviolability mean in these circumstances? Little attention was paid to these considerations during the preparation of the Article, perhaps on the hopeful ground that the circumstances involved represented only a small proportion of the cases likely to arise. Whilst the issue raised does not permit of a categorical answer, unless at the least it is known more precisely how the documents came to be 'detached' from the mission, in instances where the papers, though 'official' in origin, are manifestly at variance with the legitimate functions of the mission, there is no reason in principle why they should be accorded inviolability.[2]

(b) *Correspondence.* As discussed above, the official correspondence of the mission is inviolable.[3]

(c) *Property of the mission.* In so far as property is located within mission premises it enjoys the benefits of the inviolability of the buildings themselves. Article 22, paragraph 3, provides expressly that,

[1] Article II, Section 4.

[2] Thus in *R v. Rose* [1946–7] 2 C.R. 107, [1947] 88 C.C.C. and a series of related Canadian decisions, documents brought by a Russian defector from the USSR Mission in Ottawa, showing the existence of an espionage network, were used in evidence—and constituted indeed the main item in the prosecution. A plea of 'inviolability' with respect to the documents was rejected. See Cohen, 'Espionage and Immunity—Some Recent Problems and Developments', *British Year Book of International Law*, xxv (1948), p. 404. The authenticity of the documents was not denied.

[3] Article 27, paragraph 2. See p. 39 above.

besides the premises themselves, the 'furniture and other property thereon' shall be immune from 'search, requisition, attachment or execution'. A similar immunity, in this case not limited to its being within the premises, is granted to the mission's means of transport. In view of the wider terms in which inviolability is extended to the property of diplomatic agents, it may be presumed that Article 22, paragraph 3, is merely intended to illustrate the inviolability of all items of property held by the mission, so as to include, for example, a bank account maintained in the name of the mission.

(*d*) *Property of diplomatic agents.* The 'papers, correspondence' and, subject to certain exceptions, the 'property' of diplomatic agents,[1] are granted inviolability under Article 30, paragraph 2. In its commentary[2] on this provision the International Law Commission made it clear that the movable property concerned was primarily that in the agent's private residence, but also included his car, his bank account, and other goods required for his personal use or essential to his livelihood. So far as bank accounts were concerned, the Commission stated that it had chiefly in mind immunity from measures of restriction, attachment or execution.[3]

A separate issue, not touched on in the Convention, concerns the difficult question of the interest which the diplomat is required to have in the property in order that he may claim inviolability, including immunity in respect of judicial proceedings, with regard to it. In *The Amazone*,[4] a case in which possession of a yacht was contested between a diplomat and his wife, the Court of Appeal held that immunity extended to all actions, including those in which title to goods was in dispute.

Personal inviolability

The obligation of the receiving State to ensure the personal inviolability of diplomatic agents and others is intended to preserve the

---

[1] For the position in respect of other categories see p. 75 ff. below.

[2] *Yearbook of the International Law Commission, 1958*, vol. II, p. 98.

[3] As in the case of *In re Ledoux, Annual Digest*, 1943–5, p. 241. There was some discussion in the International Law Commission as to whether the bank account of a diplomatic agent, besides being inviolable, was also to be given immunity from exchange control restrictions. Most members of the Commission considered that, within limits, diplomats should enjoy some freedom from exchange controls, although there was no clear agreement as to the extent of this freedom. See *Yearbook of the International Law Commission, 1958*, vol. II, pp. 145–6.

On the question of measures of execution, see generally pp. 67–8 below.

[4] [1939] P. p. 322, [1940] P. p. 40.

individuals concerned from measures of direct coercion. There is an overlap between some of the acts of restraint imposed on the host authorities under this heading and those incumbent on the receiving State as part of the immunity to be accorded from criminal jurisdiction;[1] a receiving State may not arrest or detain a protected member of the mission on either ground.[2] Nevertheless the two categories are distinct in their object: the one is primarily directed to the action (or non-action) of the courts, while 'inviolability' has as its first concern the preservation of mission staff from immediate physical harm or constraint. Accordingly, after the statement of principle, 'The person of a diplomatic agent shall be inviolable', Article 29 of the Vienna Convention continues:

He shall not be liable to any form of arrest or detention. The receiving State shall treat him with due respect and shall take all appropriate steps to prevent any attack on his person, freedom or dignity.

The restrictions on the police power of the receiving State under this provision have caused relatively little difficulty, or at least relatively little legal difficulty. If for any reason the local authorities do happen to detain someone, only to discover that he is a member of a diplomatic mission, they are usually at pains to release him as soon as possible. The matter is somewhat more complicated where the police know beforehand that the person concerned is a diplomat. If there is sufficient time to notify the ambassador in order that he may take the appropriate action, so well and good, but supposing this is not possible—if, for example, the diplomat is endangering the immediate physical safety of members of the public? In extreme cases of this kind the receiving State may be expected to take the steps necessary to prevent the diplomat from committing crimes or offences. Neither the International Law Commission nor the Vienna Conference wished, however, to introduce any express exceptions to the general principle of the inviolability of members of mission staff from arrest or detention, thus following the same attitude as was adopted in the case of the inviolability of premises and property. As regards the degree of protection to be afforded from the acts of ordinary individuals, the International Law Commission declared that the duty of the receiving State may extend to the taking of

[1] Article 31, paragraph 1. See p. 56 below.
[2] For this reason many books do not distinguish the two categories or derive the one from the other. The Vienna Conference and the International Law Commission proceeded on the assumption that executive acts such as arrest or detention were to be classified under the right to inviolability.

special measures (for example, the provision of a guard where circumstances so require), thereby endorsing the opinion by the Special
Committee of Jurists following the 'Corfu Incident' of 1923, that
'special vigilance' must be exercised in order to protect foreigners
having a 'recognized public character'.[1] As evidence of the steps
taken to fulfil their obligations in this regard, a number of States have
adopted legislation providing that persons guilty of attacks on diplomats shall be subject to severe punishment.[2] There is, however, no
formal international requirement[3] that national law shall provide an
especially heavy penalty for the infliction of physical harm on diplomats, English law for example does not do so,[4] and it is difficult to
see how such an enactment could properly be applied, except *in
terrorem*. Assuming the existence of an adequate system of criminal
law, can it be said that a man who injures a diplomat, not knowing
he is a diplomat, is nevertheless liable to a punishment in excess of
that normally given in cases of the same kind? At the very least, it
is submitted, the act must have been committed knowingly if an
extra penalty is to be justified.

JURISDICTIONAL IMMUNITY

General

In so far as much of diplomatic law depends directly on executive
action it is relatively simple in its legal structure, however complex
the political reasoning which may lie behind particular decisions
taken. In the case of jurisdictional immunity, however, the situation
is more elaborate, involving, as it does, such issues as the relationship between the executive and the courts, the interpretation by the
judiciary of the obligations incurred internationally by the executive
branch of the government, and, to a lesser extent, the interaction
between the two 'legal districts', namely that of the receiving and of
the sending State. The context of jurisdictional immunity is therefore

---

[1] League of Nations, *Official Journal* (1924), p. 524.

[2] E.g. *United States Code*, Title 18, Chapter 7, Section 112. The defence of self-
defence may be pleaded against diplomats.

[3] Cf. *Respublica v. de Longchamps* (1784), 1 Dall. p. 111: 'The person of a public
minister is sacred and inviolable. Whoever offers any violence to him, not only
affronts the sovereign he represents, but also hurts the common safety and well-
being of nations; he is guilty of a crime against the whole world.'

[4] Cf. Oppenheim, *International Law* (8 ed., 1955), vol. I, p. 789, on the evidence
of Stephen, *Digest of Criminal Law*, and the Act of Anne. See generally Lyons,
'Personal Immunities of Diplomatic Agents', *British Year Book of International
Law*, XXXI (1954), pp. 301–2.

one in which a number of legal elements may need to be considered, in the course of the intricate process whereby the normal operation of the national legal system is brought into line with the privileged status accorded to diplomatic envoys and others.[1]

The immunity conferred is primarily, though not exclusively, procedural in character. As was said in the classic judgement of *Dickinson* ✓ *v. Del Solar*, 'Diplomatic privilege does not import immunity from legal liability, but only exemption from local jurisdiction.'[2] Subject to exceptions as regards the official role he is called upon to perform in compliance with the orders of his Government, a diplomatic agent is under an obligation to observe the laws of the State receiving him[3] —or those portions of it at least which normally apply to persons (whether or not nationals) ordinarily resident within the jurisdiction. He cannot vote, he does not pay taxes, but is subject to the same injunctions to obey policemen, not to commit theft and to abide by his contracts, as anyone else, despite the fact that action cannot be taken through the courts, either by the receiving State or by a private individual, if he fails to honour these responsibilities. Immunity from jurisdiction, then, denotes essentially immunity from curial control— from the form of restraint which involvement, in any capacity (though most obviously in that of accused or defendant) in a case before the courts may entail. The immunity, which extends to all jurisdictions, criminal, civil or administrative, is enjoyed in full only by diplomatic agents accredited to the State in question; action cannot be brought against them either in respect of their own acts, nor can attempts be made to sue the Government or State concerned through the person of its envoy.

When a case involving a plea of diplomatic immunity is presented the court concerned is faced with a double task: firstly, it must ascertain whether the person claiming immunity is in fact so entitled; and, secondly, the court must rule as to the legal consequences of a successful claim. As regards the former, the problem involved is one which occurs in several contexts in the law of diplomatic privileges and immunities, namely, exactly what degree of proof is required and by what means must the diplomat show that he has the privilege he claims? Is it sufficient that he asserts title over a given piece of property, for example, for it to enjoy immunity, or must he demonstrate proof? Or is possession sufficient? In the case of personal immunity from jurisdiction, is the court bound to accord this *ab initio*,

---

[1] For the position in respect of non-diplomatic categories see p. 75 ff. below.
[2] [1930] 1 K.B. p. 376.   [3] Article 41, paragraph 1.

so as to bar any legal process, or is it a 'privilege' which must be claimed in order to be effective? The doctrine on this point is not entirely clear, if only because the position varies from country to country and any discussion eventually involves examination of the *minutiae* of the legal procedure of individual States. In France, for example, since the immunity from jurisdiction of diplomatic agents is considered a principle touching *l'ordre public*, an exemption based on that immunity must, in case of need, be stated by the jurisdiction seized.[1] The standard practice, however, is for the court to seek the advice of the executive and thus preserve the unified face which States like to maintain in their exterior contacts. Usually presented, at least in common law practice, in the form of a 'certificate' from the foreign ministry,[2] the statement of the executive sets out the facts within its competence, in particular the vital issue of whether the Government of the receiving State has recognized, or continues to recognize, the official status of the person concerned. As was said by Lord Phillimore, the certificate is not a piece of hearsay evidence but a statement of what the Foreign Office has done.[3] For English law at least the question of the extent, if any, to which the courts may go behind this statement is settled by Section 4 of the Diplomatic Privileges Act, 1964, which provides that a certificate issued by or under the authority of the Secretary of State for Foreign Affairs shall be 'conclusive evidence' of 'any fact' which is stated therein 'relating to the question whether or not a person is entitled to any privilege or immunity' under the Act. Although the terms of the executive statement may thus preclude the exercise of any wide discretion, it still remains for the courts, and not for the executive, to give a final ruling as to the consequences, in terms of local law, of the immunity afforded. Besides considering the substantive content of the immunity—an important issue in view of the various degrees of exemption accorded to the different categories of staff under the Convention—the courts may accordingly need to examine the temporal scope of the immunity,[4] the terms of any waiver made, and the

---

[1] Kiss, op. cit., nos. 601–3, p. 340.

[2] See the various articles by Lyons, *British Year Book of International Law*, XXIII (1946), p. 240; XXIV (1947), p. 116; XXVI (1949), p. 180; and XXIX (1952), p. 227; Cardozo, 'Judicial Deference to State Department Suggestions: Recognition of Prerogative or Abdication to Usurper', *Cornell L.Q.*, 48 (1963), p. 461; and Vallat, *International Law and the Practitioner* (1966), p. 51. Information given to the parties by the foreign ministry may also be accepted by the Courts.

[3] *Engelke v. Musmann* [1928] A.C. p. 433, at p. 451.

[4] See p. 80 below.

effect of any judgements given elsewhere relating to the diplomatic agent concerned.[1]

Assuming the courts of the receiving State decide that they are unable to exercise jurisdiction (or, to place the matter in the usual perspective, assuming the would-be plaintiff is advised in advance that the courts will so rule), two alternative courses may be pursued. Firstly, although exempt from the jurisdiction of the receiving State, members of the mission staff remain subject to the jurisdiction of the courts of their own country. Accordingly, though there are usually many practical, and often some legal, obstacles, it is possible for an aggrieved plaintiff from the receiving State to carry the battle to a forum where the defendant cannot claim any special status. The inadequacies of this procedure, as a method of redress of routine private claims, do not need to be stressed. The International Law Commission conceded, though with some reluctance, that sending States are not subject to an international obligation to exercise jurisdiction in cases relating to their diplomats; thus, although an action may be brought before the courts of the sending State, the outcome will depend on the normal operation of the law of the land. Courts in common law countries, for example, do not in general have jurisdiction over crimes committed abroad, and in civil cases the effect of the conflict of laws may make it impossible to give judgement unless the action has previously been heard by a court in the receiving State. Furthermore it will usually be difficult to serve legal process on a diplomat who remains *en poste*. Unless, therefore, States are prepared where necessary to adopt special legislation and to provide special courts, an effective remedy will often not be obtained even if the plaintiff goes to the expense of bringing his case in the sending State. Confronted with these difficulties and realizing that States would be reluctant to make structural changes in their legal systems (especially for so small a group of people), the International Law Commission eventually decided merely to enunciate the general principle, that immunity from the jurisdiction of the receiving State does not *per se* grant exemption from the jurisdiction of the sending State, without saying more. This decision was endorsed without change by the Vienna Conference.[2]

[1] *Salm v. Frazier, Annual Digest*, 1933–4, p. 379. The Convention of 12 June 1961 between the United Kingdom and Norway relating to reciprocal enforcement of civil judgements, distinguishes between exceptions to such enforcement on grounds of immunity under public international law and exceptions based on public policy generally. *United Nations Treaty Series*, vol. 424, p. 173.

[2] Article 31, paragraph 4.

More commonly, when a claim arises which, in the absence of immunity, would present no special features, the private citizen, or his lawyer, first writes to the member of the mission staff concerned. If he fails to obtain redress (which is not usually the case since, if only to avoid publicity and to prevent a complaint being made to his superiors, the official will attempt to settle the matter if he can), the citizen may then address himself to the head of mission. At that stage he may also try to persuade the foreign ministry of his country to take up the matter. Whether they will do so or not will be a matter for their discretion; normally they will be reluctant to intervene on the ground that their action may be harmful to the friendly relations which the two States enjoy. If the ministry is prepared to pursue the claim it may, like the private claimant, either seek to obtain an admission of liability and payment of any sums due, or waiver of the immunity so that the case may be settled by the competent court. If the negotiations through diplomatic channels do not succeed, the receiving State may possibly go to the length of declaring the member of mission staff *persona non grata*.

Thus an 'executive style' procedure exists, not always very effective so far as the individual plaintiff is concerned, parallel to that which would normally be available through the courts. The root principle involved was admirably summarized nearly a century ago by Sir Robert Phillimore:

The object of international law, in this as in other matters, is not to work injustice, not to prevent the enforcement of a just demand, but to substitute negotiations between governments, though they may be dilatory and the issue distant and uncertain, for the ordinary use of courts of justice in cases where such use would lessen the dignity or embarrass the function of the representatives of a foreign State.[1]

Material content

(*a*) *Immunity from criminal jurisdiction*. That ambassadors and members of the suite should be exempt from criminal jurisdiction has been accepted law since the seventeenth century. In a celebrated group of cases which occurred during the Elizabethan and early Stuart period involving charges of treason and other 'state' offences there was some doubt in the minds of those consulted as to whether legal immunity was due as of right, or whether jurisdiction might be exercised, if the receiving sovereign so chose, in order to punish such

---

[1] *The Charkieh* (1873) L.R. 4 A. and E. p. 59, at p. 97.

heinous crimes;[1] in none of these cases, however, was any action taken against the diplomat involved except to require him to leave the country. It remained for Grotius to sum up the basic reason for the modern principle: 'the security of ambassadors outweighs any advantage which accrues from a punishment.'[2] Sir Matthew Hale, writing a century later, had similarly little doubts that, faced with a choice between permitting the mutual exercise of jurisdiction over diplomats or of sending offenders back to their master, States had decided on the latter course. He wrote:

> The truth is, the business of embassadors is rather managed according to rules of prudence, and mutual concerns and temperaments among princes, where possibly a severe construction of an embassador's actions, and prosecution of them by one prince may at another time return to the like disadvantage of his own agents and embassadors; and therefore they are rather temperaments measured by politic prudence and indulgence, than according to the strict rules of reason and justice.[3]

The following official statement describing the position of diplomats in France may be taken as exemplifying present-day practice:

> . . . les agents diplomatiques échappent à toute application de la loi pénale française, qu'ils puissent être inculpés comme auteurs, coauteurs ou complices et quelle que soit la nature de l'infraction relevée contravention, délit, crime, soit contre des particuliers, soit contre la sûreté ou le crédit de l'Etat.[4]

The requirement that diplomatic agents should be exempt from criminal jurisdiction has been observed with exceptional strictness. Hurst states that there is no precedent in which a diplomatic agent was made subject, without his consent, to the criminal jurisdiction of the

---

[1] See the Opinion of the Doctors in the case of *Leslie, Bishop of Ross* (1571). The advice given in *Marche's Case* (1615), that an ambassador was immune from punishment for a breach of positive law but might be prosecuted for an offence against the 'law of nature or reason' indicates the line of argument used and the surviving relics of mediaeval unity. McNair, *International Law Opinions* (1956), vol. I, pp. 186–7.

[2] As he added, '. . . since the views of those who send the ambassadors are generally different from the views of those who receive them, and often directly opposed, it is scarcely possible that in every case something may not be said against an ambassador which shall present the appearance of a crime. And although some things are so obvious that they do not admit of doubt, yet the universal peril is sufficient to establish the justice and advantage of the universal law.' *De Jure Belli ac Pacis, Libri Tres* (1646), bk II, ch. XVIII, 4 (*Classics of International Law*, 1925), p. 443.

[3] *Historia Placitorum Coronae* (1736), vol. I, p. 98.

[4] United Nations Legislative Series, *Laws and Regulations Regarding Diplomatic and Consular Privileges and Immunities* (1958), vol. VII, p. 121.

receiving State.[1] Although there have been several instances since his day which could be put on the other side, the principle continues to hold firm. When serious breaches of criminal law are committed, such as the infliction of deliberate physical harm or acts of espionage, the receiving State can either ignore the fact, issue a rebuke, or proceed to declare the offender *persona non grata*. If the diplomat fails to leave the country after such a declaration, he can be brought before the courts and punished in the normal way. Unless this sequence of events occurs or unless, exceptionally, the sending State agrees to waive immunity, no criminal measures can be taken against the diplomatic agent concerned.

(b) *Immunity from civil and administrative jurisdiction*. Immunity from civil and administrative[2] jurisdiction was slower to emerge than that in respect of criminal procedures, but by the eighteenth century it too had become established in state practice. Whereas, however, the decision as to whether or not penal measures were to be initiated had lain, as it continues to do, largely in the hands of the public authorities, the possibility existed in the case of civil actions that ordinary citizens might seek to set the normal machinery of the courts in motion. It was in fact this contingency that the earliest enactments were designed to meet, so as to prevent injury to the State's external relations caused by private suits directed against ambassadors and members of their suites. That celebrated statute, now repealed, the Act of Anne,[3] was adopted in 1708 after the Russian Ambassador was placed in custody, having been taken from his coach and some of his belongings seized, in an attempt by his creditors to obtain satisfaction of their debts.[4] Although proceedings were held in the Court of Queen's Bench and before the Privy Council which resulted in the offenders being committed to prison, no sentence was passed since it could not be shown to be an offence under existing law[5] to arrest an

---

[1] *International Law, The Collected Papers of Sir Cecil Hurst* (1950), p. 217. (The statement was originally made in 1926.)

[2] The jurisdictions from which immunity is given include that of any special courts, 'e.g. commercial courts, courts set up to apply social legislation, and all administrative authorities exercising judicial functions'. *Yearbook of the International Law Commission, 1958*, vol. II, p. 98.

[3] 7 Anne, c. 12. Repealed by the Diplomatic Privileges Act, 1964, Schedule 2.

[4] De Martens, *Causes célèbres du droit des gens* (1827), tome I, pp. 47–74.

[5] Lord Mansfield in *Triquet v. Bath* (1764) 3 Burr. p. 1478, at p. 1480, declared that, since the law of nations was part of English law an infraction could be punished as a misdemeanour, but added that this punishment had not been inflicted in the Russian Ambassador's case since the penalties involved were so small that they would have constituted a fresh insult to the Czar.

ambassador for debt. In order to appease the Russian sovereign the Statute of 1708 was adopted, recalling in its preamble the behaviour of 'several turbulent and disorderly persons' who had insulted the envoy 'contrary to the law of nations and in prejudice of the rights and privileges' which ambassadors had always possessed, and declaring 'all writs and processes' whereby ambassadors, public ministers and their servants might be arrested or imprisoned, or their property seized, 'utterly null and void'. It was added that any person, including any attorney or solicitor, who attempted to sue forth or prosecute any such writ or process, might be tried before a special court consisting of the Lord Chancellor, the Keeper of the Great Seal and the Chief Justices of the Queen's Bench and Common Pleas, or any two of them, but there is no record of proceedings having ever been instituted before this body. Although statutes in similar form were repeated in other countries,[1] the development of national administration which occurred in the nineteenth century (including the appointment of regular legal advisers to the foreign ministry and the practice of submitting an executive certificate to the courts) caused these enactments to play an increasingly limited, if still important, part in overall practice.

The Vienna Convention restates the general principle, that diplomatic agents are immune from civil and administrative jurisdiction, subject to three limited exceptions as regards actions in which the diplomat may be involved in his private capacity, namely with respect to interests in real property, cases of succession, and professional or commercial activities. These exceptions, which did not form a clearly established part of prior law, are all instances in which, if the sending State did not have jurisdiction, it would be virtually impossible for any court elsewhere to examine the issue; secondly, they are all distinct from the performance of official duties; and, lastly, they do not involve, in normal circumstances, the possibility of criminal proceedings. It was the fact that these latter considerations could not easily or logically be excluded which caused the Vienna Conference to decline to adopt a Netherlands proposal whereby a fourth exception would have been added, giving the courts of the sending State jurisdiction over claims for damages arising out of traffic accidents in which a diplomatic agent was involved, unless an action could be brought directly against the insurance company.[2] It was pointed out that a considerable number of persons connected with diplomatic

---

[1] E.g. *United States Code*, Title 22, Chapter 4, Sections 252–3.
[2] A/CONF.20/C.1/L.186/Rev.1.

missions now use cars but that unless a private citizen injured in a traffic accident had a right of direct action against either the diplomat or the insurance company in the courts of the receiving State, it would be very unlikely that he would receive the compensation due to him. Recourse to diplomatic channels would be of little avail if the diplomat and his insurers denied responsibility;[1] impartial determination of the facts was essential, for unless insurance companies were given the right to dispute the facts they would be reluctant to cover the risk.[2] There was, in addition, the factor of public opinion to be considered, for the general public, and indeed members of national legislatures, had shown themselves increasingly dissatisfied with the immunity which diplomats enjoyed in traffic cases. Although the Netherlands proposal was supported by a number of countries, including Switzerland, which introduced an amendment that would have denied immunity with respect to administrative procedures for the issue or withdrawal of driving licences[3] in order to provide a sanction for persistent traffic offenders, most States were not prepared to go so far. The normal procedures, it was declared, were adequate to deal with the cases which arose. If this exception was admitted, why not others, and why not all traffic offences, not just those involving non-penal liability? The United Kingdom delegate pointed out that the Netherlands amendment, unlike the three accepted cases, dealt with a situation which might arise during performance of official duties; supposing, for example, the accident occurred whilst the diplomat was driving to the foreign ministry in order to deliver a government note? The Committee of the Whole eventually rejected both the Netherlands and the Swiss amendments by a heavy margin.[4] Despite the size of the negative vote cast, however, the fact that these proposals were made at all, and the difficulty which those speaking against them had in fully rebutting the arguments given in their favour, suggest that further inroads on the principle of immunity from civil jurisdiction may occur in future years. Although the test of 'functional necessity' supports the unimpeded use by the diplomat of his own means of transport—and we may note in passing that the ambassador's conveyance has been a frequent source of ill-feeling

---

[1] See, for example, the case cited by Kiss, op. cit., tome III, no. 595, pp. 337–8.

[2] Anxious English readers may note that insurance companies operating in the United Kingdom 'have undertaken to refrain from relying on the privileged status of a diplomatic client in motor insurance claims'. Statement of the Minister of Transport in answer to a question raised in the House of Commons, quoted in *British Practice in International Law, 1964—I* (ed. Lauterpacht), p. 74.

[3] A/CONF.20/C.1/L.215.   [4] *Official Records*, vol. I, p. 172.

since at least the seventeenth century—it is hard to believe that the immunities struck at by the Dutch and Swiss proposals have the same degree of importance as, for example, the inviolability of correspondence or immunity from criminal jurisdiction with respect to allegations of espionage. The rejection of the two suggestions did, however, spur the adoption by the Conference of a resolution, put forward by the representative of Israel, recommending that the sending State should waive immunity in respect of civil claims whenever possible and, where this was not done, that the sending State 'would use its best endeavours' to ensure that a just settlement was reached.[1]

Exceptions from immunity from civil and administrative jurisdiction

(*a*) *Exceptions ratione materiae.* The Vienna Conference agreed to accept three exceptions to the principle of immunity from civil and administrative jurisdiction.[2]

(*i*) *Real property.* In accordance with the claim of all States to exclusive jurisdiction over immovable property, 'the very substratum of national territory', as the International Law Commission called it,[3] the jurisdictional immunity of diplomatic agents does not extend to real actions concerning immovable property situated in the territory of the receiving State and which is held in a private capacity and not on behalf of the sending State for the purposes of the mission. In countries where, because of local legislation, it is necessary that title be vested in the ambassador himself, the essential requirement is that the property should be used by the mission.[4] In the event (as will often be the case) that the private property owned is also the residence of the agent, no measures of execution may be taken which infringe its inviolability;[5] thus, supposing there is a dispute as to title, the diplomat will not be able to dispute jurisdiction so as to prevent the court from giving judgement, although the possibility will be open to him, at least in theory, to deny possession to the legal owner.[6]

[1] Ibid., vol. II, p. 90. In the International Law Commission's proposals on special missions jurisdictional immunity does not extend to accidents occurring outside official functions (Article 31, paragraph 2(*d*)) and a provision is included on the settlement of civil claims (Article 42). *Report of the International Law Commission on the work of its nineteenth session, 1967, General Assembly Official Records, Twenty-second Session, Suppl. No. 9* (A/6709/Rev.1).

[2] Article 31, paragraph 1(*a*), (*b*) and (*c*).

[3] *Yearbook of the International Law Commission, 1957*, vol. II, p. 139.

[4] Sir Gerald Fitzmaurice, *Yearbook of the International Law Commission, 1957*, vol. I, p. 96.   [5] Article 31, paragraph 3.   [6] Having regard to the obligation to respect local law (Article 41, paragraph 1), any such behaviour might be expected to lead to a declaration that the individual concerned is *persona non grata*.

(*ii*) *Succession*. As every lawyer knows, actions relating to succession are frequently complex and involve the collaboration of a large number of parties. They also form a standard example of the type of case for which resort to the courts of the sending State will scarcely ever provide a practical solution. There is therefore much good sense, as well as probably new law,[1] in the second exception which declares that a diplomatic agent does not enjoy immunity from actions relating to succession in which he is involved as a private person, whether as an executor, administrator, heir or legatee.

(*iii*) *Professional and commercial activities*. In principle a diplomatic agent, or other member of a mission, is employed for that purpose and no other. To safeguard this rule, the Vienna Convention provides expressly that no diplomatic agent may act in a professional or commercial capacity for personal profit outside his official functions.[2] It comes therefore as somewhat of a surprise to find that the third exception to the principle of immunity from civil jurisdiction concerns actions 'relating to any professional or commercial activity performed by the diplomatic agent in the receiving State outside his official functions'. The explanation is twofold: firstly, the prohibition of professional and commercial activities extends only to diplomats and not to other members of mission staff or their respective families; whereas non-diplomatic members of mission staff (and their families) enjoy no immunity from civil jurisdiction in respect of such activities, the members of the family of a diplomat would have complete exemption in respect of their professional or commercial activities if this limitation were not included.[3] Secondly, the prohibition of non-diplomatic activities may possibly be set aside by the receiving State in the light of the particular circumstances, as where, for example, the diplomat has some special skill or the activity is of a limited duration. In that event the diplomat enjoys no special exemption as regards any contracts he enters into or any acts of malfeasance which he may commit.

[1] *Sed quaere*. See *Re Nijdam, International Law Reports*, 1955, p. 530, where an Austrian court required a Netherlands diplomat to supply information on the value of the estate left in the Netherlands by a person who died in Austria, leaving an estate of which the diplomat claimed a *legitima portio*.
[2] Article 42. As the United Kingdom Government pointed out on another occasion, the scope of the expression 'professional or commercial activity' is not clear. Does it cover, for instance, disputes about the ownership of, or liability for, calls on shares in a company registered in the receiving State? *Comments by Governments on the Draft Articles on Special Missions drawn up by the Commission at its Seventeenth Session*, A/CN.4/188/Add.1, 13 June 1966, p. 5.
[3] Article 37, See p. 76 ff. below.

(b) *Initiation of proceedings*. Diplomatic agents and other persons who benefit from jurisdictional immunity with respect to civil actions receive that immunity, as they receive others, in order that they may not be impeded in the free execution of their duties. That reasoning does not extend to denying them access to the courts of the receiving State (normally, it may be presumed, with the consent of the sending State) to initiate an action; in such proceedings they have the same *locus standi* as any other foreigner within the jurisdiction. Resort to court action is not therefore to be classified as an implied waiver of jurisdictional immunity but as the exercise of an entitlement which is open to them, as it is to others, in their potential capacity as individual plaintiffs. Jurisdictional immunity does, or might, come into play, however, in the event that the defendant presents a counter-claim. To guard against the unjust position which would result if, though a diplomat might bring a suit, he could plead immunity in order to rebut any counter-claim, the Vienna Convention provides expressly that, where a person benefiting from jurisdictional immunity initiates proceedings, such action precludes him from invoking that immunity 'in respect of any counter-claim directly connected with the principal claim'.[1] The acceptance of the jurisdiction of the receiving State is deemed to have been made 'as fully as may be required to settle the dispute in all stages closely linked to the basic claim',[2] and thus includes such related matters as the production of documents and the giving of evidence, in so far as these may be necessary for the determination of the case. Technically, however, the resort by the diplomat to the courts of the receiving State relates only to acceptance of jurisdiction *per se*; he remains immune, even in these circumstances, for measures of execution, for which an express waiver is required from the Government of the sending State.[3] It may be presumed that such a waiver will normally be made if the diplomat does not voluntarily settle any judgement given against him.

Waiver of immunity

In addition to the exceptions noted above, the jurisdiction of the receiving State may also be exercised if the Government of the sending State agrees to waive the immunity of its employee. The waiver given, moreover, though confined to the particular case, may extend to any branch of jurisdiction, criminal no less than civil, from which the diplomat otherwise enjoys immunity.

---

[1] Article 32, paragraphs 1 and 2.   [3] Article 32, paragraph 4.
[2] *Yearbook of the International Law Commission, 1957*, vol. II, p. 140.

The Vienna Conference was at pains to emphasize that waiver can only be made by the Government of the sending State and must at all times be express.[1] The latter requirement constitutes a change in established practice where it had become established that, although mere non-appearance did not constitute acceptance of the court's jurisdiction, certain acts, such as active participation in an action, might be so interpreted. The distinction which the International Law Commission sought to draw between criminal proceedings (in which waiver was required to be express) and civil proceedings (where waiver might be implied)[2] was not accepted by the Conference. It is not essential, however, that the waiver be conveyed by a communication sent between Governments; a waiver by the head of mission will be deemed to be a waiver by the State concerned.[3]

The effect of a waiver, once given, has been obscured in English practice by the wording of the Act of Anne which declared 'null and void' any writs or processes issued against diplomatic envoys. If this was indeed the case, how did a waiver breathe life into a still-born action? In 1965 the Court of Appeal gave the straightforward interpretation that actions brought against members of mission staff are to be regarded as voidable, not void; how otherwise, as the court pointed out, could waiver give jurisdiction? 'What is null and void is not a phoenix, there are no ashes from which it can be brought to life.'[4] The act of waiving immunity proceeds, therefore, on the basis that the courts will be competent to exercise jurisdiction in the case in question, as in any other, once the procedural bar has been removed.

Immunity in respect of acts performed in the exercise of official functions

The immunity from jurisdiction enjoyed by diplomatic agents, though received by virtue of their office, contrasts sharply with the immunity which is granted to members of mission staff in respect of acts performed in the course of their official duties. Whereas immunity from jurisdiction normally extends to all activities, both public and private, the other relates specifically to those connected with the functions of the various categories of persons concerned. Furthermore, although in principle jurisdictional immunity lasts only so long as the diplomat occupies his post and ceases when the diplomat leaves, immunity in respect of official acts is subject to no such temporal limitation—

[1] Article 32, paragraphs 1 and 2.
[2] *Yearbook of the International Law Commission, 1958*, vol. II, p. 99.
[3] Section 2(3), Diplomatic Privileges Act, 1964.
[4] *Empson v. Smith* [1965] 2 All E.R. p. 881, at p. 887 (Diplock L.J.).

indeed, it is often only after jurisdictional immunity has ended that this immunity is clearly visible.[1] Lastly, in the case of some (and they the most important) acts performed in execution of official duties, the member of the mission staff enjoys not merely immunity from court proceedings but also immunity from the obligations of the law of the receiving State: in other words, exemption from law as well as from jurisdiction.

As regards the categories of persons receiving this immunity, these include, besides diplomatic agents, members of the administrative and technical staff whose immunity from civil and administrative jurisdiction does not extend to 'acts performed outside the course of their duties';[2] members of the service staff, who receive immunity 'in respect of acts performed in the course of their duties';[3] and, finally, diplomatic agents who are nationals of or permanently resident in the receiving State, who 'enjoy only immunity from jurisdiction, and inviolability, in respect of official acts performed in the exercise of (their) functions'.[4] In these cases, as opposed to that of a normal diplomatic agent, it is therefore of the essence to determine the scope of the duties performed if any action is brought; only if it is shown that the act complained of was done in the exercise of official functions will the courts of the receiving State be barred from proceeding to consider the case. The Convention does not say who is to make this determination, nor whether it is to be shaped to the individual defendant, i.e. an extreme functional test, or whether it is to be related to the general category of staff of which the defendant is a member. Whilst it would be improper to require the sending State to go into court and demonstrate in detail how the act in question fell within the range of duties ascribed to the particular person concerned, on the other hand, there is no reason why the bare assertion of that State should be regarded as sufficient in itself to prevent the court from giving its ruling. The certificate of the executive furthermore, though conclusive as regards the facts stated, may not cover the entire range of issues,[5] thus leaving a considerable area for the determination of the court.

---

[1] Article 39, paragraph 2. See *Zoernsch v. Waldock* [1964] 2 All E.R. p. 256, especially at p. 261 (Wilmer L.J.).

[2] Article 37, paragraph 2. [3] Article 37, paragraph 3.

[4] Article 38, paragraph 1. It is a nice point to distinguish what difference in substance there is between the three formulations just cited.

[5] See the discussion in the House of Commons during the Second Reading of the future Diplomatic Privileges Act, when it was presumed that the head of mission would certify whether or not members of service staff were on duty in traffic cases. *British Practice in International Law, 1964—II* (ed. Lauterpacht), pp. 219-21.

As regards the extent of the immunity which is afforded, there is a degree of uncertainty as to whether immunity 'in respect of acts performed in the course of . . . duties' or 'in the exercise of . . . functions' comprises: (*a*) solely official acts in the strictest sense, namely the job the official was employed to perform and no other (such as, for example, the actual dispatch and receipt of messages by a wireless operator); (*b*) acts in close connexion with the above, so as to include, for example, a traffic accident which occurs whilst the person is driving to the foreign ministry on official business; or (*c*), acts which occur 'in the course of . . . duties' in a looser, temporal sense. The last category can probably be dismissed; if the draftsmen of the Vienna Convention had meant to say this they would have used different language. The major difficulty centres over the cases falling under the second heading.[1] The *travaux préparatoires* are susceptible of interpretation either way. It is submitted, on a basis of 'the reason of the thing', that the higher the official the more likely it is that immunity will be accorded in respect of incidents in the second category. However, in so far as the immunity is directed to acts rather than to persons, even this is not entirely certain. At all events, if in future years national courts, aided by their respective foreign ministries, seek to impose the test of functional necessity in all its potential vigour, their interpretation of this issue will be one of the principal means available to them.

There is, lastly, the question whether immunity in respect of acts performed in the exercise of official functions differs in quality from jurisdictional immunity. It is evident that in the case of certain activities the only factor which prevents courts of the receiving State from exercising jurisdiction is the personal immunity which the diplomat or other members of the mission staff enjoys. In a perfectly routine claim—money owed by a diplomat for the purchase of household goods or with respect to a garage bill, for example—the court will be unable to try the action unless the Government of the sending State agrees to waive the immunity. In the case of 'acts performed in the course of . . . duties' or 'in the exercise of . . . functions', on the other hand, this may or may not be the case. In the event of a traffic accident whilst driving to the foreign ministry, the local courts would normally be competent until immunity is pleaded. But what about,

[1] See van Panhuys, 'In the Borderland between the Act of State Doctrine and Questions of Jurisdictional Immunities', *International and Comparative Law Quarterly*, 13 (1964), p. 1193, and Dinstein, 'Diplomatic Immunity from Jurisdiction Ratione Materiae', ibid., 15 (1966), p. 76.

say, the refusal of a passport, or the dismissal of a member of mission staff? In these instances the courts of the receiving State would lack jurisdiction, even if the case was entrusted to them, on the grounds that the matters concerned are administrative acts of a foreign State which are not subject to the 'appreciation' of the courts of another State.[1] Furthermore the legislatures of receiving States are obliged to refrain from the adoption of measures designed to control acts of the kind in question, or conferring the requisite competence on their courts, unless, at the least, a special treaty has been concluded between the two States. We strike here at one of those facts of international life which characterize the system of independent national States, namely the separation of powers, as well as of jurisdictions, between individual countries.

Ancillary immunities

(a) *Immunity from giving evidence.* In addition to being immune from jurisdiction as a defendant or with respect to criminal proceedings, a diplomatic agent 'is not obliged to give evidence as a witness'.[2] During the 1958 session of the International Law Commission there was a long debate as to whether this rule should be modified to take account of the three exceptions referred to in Article 31, paragraph 1. It was eventually decided that, since in these cases the diplomat would be engaged in a private capacity, it could be left to him to decide whether to go into court, and to accept the consequences if he failed to do so; it was, furthermore, debatable whether it was correct to speak of an obligation to give evidence *qua* witness in a case where the agent was himself a party.

As regards the more general aspects, the requirement that diplomatic agents should respect local law necessitated, in the opinion of the International Law Commission, that the agent ought to co-operate with the local authorities, particularly as regards any criminal activities which he had witnessed.[3] Some countries, moreover, had special rules regarding the manner in which diplomats might give evidence, for example by answering written questions or by submission of an affidavit, so as to render it unnecessary for them to appear in court or to be cross-examined.

(b) *Immunity from measures of execution.* The immunity enjoyed by

[1] See Niboyet, 'Immunité de juridiction et incompétence d'attribution', *Revue critique de droit international privé*, xxxix (1950), p. 139.
[2] Article 31, paragraph 2.
[3] *Yearbook of the International Law Commission, 1958*, vol. ii, p. 98.

diplomatic agents from measures of execution is stated twice, in two different ways. Article 31, paragraph 3, provides that no measures of execution may be taken against a diplomatic agent except in respect of cases coming under the exceptions listed in paragraph 1 of that Article, and even then, subject to the condition, 'that the measures concerned can be taken without infringing the inviolability of his person or of his residence'. Thus, once out of its garage, a diplomat's motor car may conceivably be seized in execution of a debt incurred under one of these headings, for all that he may continue to need it in order to do his job.[1] Secondly, Article 32, paragraph 4, declares that any waiver of immunity from civil or administrative proceedings is not to be held to imply waiver of immunity in respect of the execution of the judgement, for which a separate waiver must be made.

[1] Article 30, paragraph 2, provides for the inviolability of the property of a diplomatic agent 'except as provided in paragraph 3 of Article 31'.

Chapter IV

REMAINING ISSUES RELATING TO DIPLOMATIC MISSIONS: SPECIAL MISSIONS

FISCAL AND PARAFISCAL IMMUNITIES

ALTHOUGH it is commonly stated that diplomatic missions and their personnel are immune from the fiscal laws of the receiving State, the books do not usually proceed to describe how this exemption is actually applied. The reason for this omission lies in the fact that the immunity in question requires interpretation in terms of local law; the customary rule, acknowledged in outline, lacks uniformity since its application in any given case depends on the tax structure of the particular State concerned. In the circumstances it is not surprising that the principle was often said to rest on courtesy and reciprocity;[1] unless the latter safeguard were maintained a receiving State could not be sure of getting its money's worth of exemptions for its own mission. Whilst the Vienna Convention has not ended this situation in its entirety, the act of codification has served to place the immunities concerned on a more precise and definite footing than hitherto. The process of determining the new law entailed in fact an exercise in comparative jurisprudence which was the reverse of that which a municipal lawyer, called upon to interpret the previous customary rule, was required to perform. Whereas the latter, whether a judge, a solicitor, or the legal adviser to the ministry of finance, sought to deduce from a broad principle that a specific immunity was or was not to be granted, the process of codification involved the search for general terms which would mark off the respective spheres of fiscal competence of the two States and define, in adequate detail, the different categories of taxes from which it was desired to give exemption. Although the municipal lawyer will continue to be concerned with evaluating and characterizing particular national laws against the principles established internationally, he will henceforth

[1] See the original report of the Special Rapporteur, *Yearbook of the International Law Commission, 1955*, vol. II, p. 16, paragraphs 55-6. Note also the USSR Statute of 1 June 1966, concerning diplomatic and consular missions, Articles 10 and 16. *International Legal Materials*, v (1966), pp. 804, 806.

have the advantage of an express statement of the content of the relevant international obligations.

The immunities comprised under this heading may be divided into three groups: immunity from taxation in the usual sense; immunity from customs duties; and immunity from various other charges and obligations, including social security provisions.

Immunity from taxation

(*a*) *The mission.* The mission (or, more strictly, the sending State in the form of the mission) is exempt from the fiscal laws of the receiving State which are designed to raise revenues for that State or its component parts. If this were not the case not only would one State be given power to tax the assets of another, but the functioning of the mission might itself be made subject to interference at the hands of the authorities of the receiving State. Although it was regarded as so self-evident as scarcely to require inclusion, Article 28 provides expressly that no taxation may be imposed on the fees anc charges levied by the mission in the course of its official duties. In addition, no dues or taxes, whether 'national, regional or municipal' are payable by the sending State or the head of mission in respect of the premises used by the mission.[1] This last exemption does not extend to cover the cost of 'specific services', such as the provision of water, gas and electricity, since in these instances the payment made does not constitute a tax but represents the charge made for the commodity actually supplied to the mission.

The immunity from taxation which is afforded in respect of mission premises is dependent on the occupation and use of the premises concerned for mission purposes, not on actual ownership by the sending State. That State may therefore claim exemption even where it only rents or leases the premises unless the owner has specified in the contract that any taxes falling due are to be paid by the mission. In this event the obligation assumed by the mission becomes part of the consideration paid and usually involves, in effect, not the payment of taxes as such but an increase in the overall rent.[2] The Convention provides expressly that persons contracting with the sending State or the head of the mission cannot themselves claim the benefit of the exemption from taxation which is given,[3] thus preserving, lest

[1] Article 23, paragraph 1.
[2] *Yearbook of the International Law Commission, 1958*, vol. II, p. 96. See also the legal opinion given by the United Nations Secretariat, *United Nations Juridical Yearbook, 1964*, p. 226.
[3] Article 23, paragraph 2.

there should be any doubt in the matter, the principle that only the intended beneficiaries are to be accorded immunity.

(b) *Mission staff*. A diplomatic agent is exempt from the taxation laws of the receiving State, whether 'personal or real, national, regional or municipal', as the Vienna Convention puts it.[1] The basic reason for this exemption, as in the case of all special exemptions granted to diplomats, is the prohibition of interference by the receiving State: *ne impediatur legatio*. Besides this, the most fundamental consideration, it should be borne in mind that, as officials of another State (to whose tax laws they are subject) and having no vote or other means of direct participation in civic life, their privilege has no anti-social connotation—it indicates instead the independence of the different national States involved. On consideration, too, of some of the administrative problems of attempting to tax diplomatic agents—the frequency with which they change posts, the need to assess their expenses, the difficulty of taking action in the event of non-compliance—it is clear that short of a radical change in the attitude of States to another, the present position is likely to continue.

The broad principle of the immunity from taxation enjoyed by diplomats and others[2] is nevertheless subject to certain exceptions which are consolidated in Article 34 of the Vienna Convention. These modifications are of some technicality and can only be noticed here in passing; in general, the exceptions listed concern the diplomat in his private capacity. Diplomatic agents are not exempt, firstly, from indirect taxes 'of a kind which are normally incorporated in the price of goods or services'.[3] I know of no study which establishes what taxes are incorporated by most States in the price of goods or services, nor does the Convention in its *travaux préparatoires* define what is meant by an 'indirect tax', or who is to say that it is indirect. Is the ruling of the tax-levying authority to apply, or is resort to be had (which, it is submitted, would be more correct) to a comparative approach? Secondly, a diplomatic agent is not exempt from dues or taxes on private immovable property which he holds on his own behalf—a logical corollary of the absence of immunity from jurisdiction in respect of actions relating to such property.[4] In

[1] Article 34.   [2] For the position as regards other categories see p. 75 ff. below.
[3] Article 34(a). When signing the Convention Japan made the following declaration: 'It is understood that the taxes referred to in Article 34(a) include those collected by special collectors under the laws and regulations of Japan provided that they are eventually incorporated in the price of goods and services', and gave as an example the payment by passengers of 'travelling tax' when buying tickets from railway, shipping and airline companies for travel in Japan.
[4] Article 31, paragraph 1(a).

addition, subject to the provisions of Article 23 relating to the immunity from taxation enjoyed in respect of mission premises,[1] a diplomatic agent does not enjoy immunity from official charges connected with immovable property, such as court or record fees, mortgage dues and stamp duty.[2] The Article also provides that agents shall be obliged to pay for 'specific services rendered'; although this is primarily directed to charges for public utilities it may cover other acts or services provided directly for the diplomat, for example, charges for permission to install or operate a wireless or television receiver.[3]

Lastly, diplomatic agents and others connected with a mission do not enjoy exemption from estate, succession or inheritance duties except as regards movable property which is in the receiving State owing to the presence there of the deceased as a member of the mission or as the member of the family of a member,[4] nor are they immune from taxation on 'private income having its source in the receiving State and capital taxes on investments made in commercial undertakings in the receiving State'. The latter possibility, though having some basis in earlier practice, represents one of the definite if minor changes introduced by the Vienna Convention. The imposition of 'capital taxes on investments' is relatively straightforward but taxing 'private income having its source in the receiving State' may be more complicated. What account is to be taken of his official salary and expenses in estimating the tax payable on income from other sources? Such questions are left for discussion between foreign ministries, in consultation with the local tax authority.

Immunity from customs duties

As regards customs exemptions, the Vienna Convention has codified and made law what was previously an uncertain, though widespread, practice, often said to be resting solely on courtesy and not due as of right to individual diplomats. Henceforth receiving States are obliged to permit the entry of articles imported for the official use of the mission or for the personal use of the diplomat or his household, and to grant such articles exemption from all customs duties, taxes and related charges (other than those for storage, cartage and similar services).[5] In order to guard against abuse, the receiving State is,

---

[1] This qualification only applies to the head of mission.   [2] Article 34(*f*).
[3] Delegate of Austria, *Official Records*, vol. I, p. 186.
[4] Article 39, paragraph 4. This does not apply if the deceased was a national of, or permanently resident in, the receiving State.
[5] Article 36, paragraph 1.

however, permitted to adopt laws or regulations governing the manner in which the privileges concerned may be exercised; by way of illustration the International Law Commission mentioned the restrictions which may be placed on the quantity of goods imported or on the period during which goods imported duty-free may not be resold.[1]

Article 36 further provides that the personal baggage of a diplomatic agent may be inspected if there are serious grounds for believing that it contains articles which are not for personal or official use or whose import or export is prohibited by the law or controlled by the quarantine regulations of the receiving State; such inspection as the authorities of the receiving State may conduct must, however, be carried out only in the presence of the agent himself or of his authorized representative. Clauses such as this illustrate, in a very limited but specific way, the extent to which States are, in their mutual dealings, dependent on one another. Paragraph 4 of Article 36 states the general rule, that personal baggage may not be inspected, and permits exceptions only where there are 'serious grounds' for presuming that the baggage contains prohibited articles. Supposing one receiving State begins to find 'serious grounds' in the case of all diplomats? Or of all the diplomats of a particular country? What constitutes 'serious grounds'? In the circumstances likely to prevail, unless the belief is borne out by the inspection, the receiving State will be reluctant to specify either what its suspicions were, or its sources of information. Thus, if receiving States are dependent on individual diplomats not to transport illicit goods, all States *qua* sending States are dependent, in a wider sense, on the exercise by receiving States of their powers with a due sense of responsibility and not merely of local authority.

Immunity from personal services and social security provisions

Ordinary citizens of a country, and even those who, though of another nationality, have made their homes there, may rightly be called upon to respond to communal needs: to perform jury service, for example, to be conscripted in the army, or to help meet a public emergency, such as a flood or forest fire. Although circumstances may well arise when, out of sheer humanity or for the sake of good relations, a diplomat or his Government may decide that the mission and its staff should assist in these undertakings, such action cannot be rendered compulsory by the receiving State. The accepted rule, as

[1] *Yearbook of the International Law Commission, 1958*, vol. II, p. 100.

stated in the Vienna Convention, declares that the receiving country is obliged to exempt diplomatic agents from 'all personal services, from all public service of all kind whatsoever, and from military obligations, such as those connected with requisitioning, military contributions and billeting'.[1]

Whereas these 'traditional' cases are susceptible of a relatively straightforward solution, the question of participation in national social security schemes requires a careful balance to be struck between the independence of the diplomatic agent and the need, accepted by all modern societies, to provide an adequate measure of social security for their citizens. In the case of members of the staff of the mission and their families,[2] it is presumed that they will be covered by the scheme maintained by the sending State: even if this should not be so, they are exempt from the social security provisions in force in the receiving country.[3] A similar exemption extends to the private servants of diplomatic agents, provided these are not nationals of, or permanently resident in, the receiving State, and are covered by the social security scheme in force in the sending State or in a third State.[4] If these conditions are not met the diplomat who employs the servant is required to observe the obligations which the relevant legislation of the receiving State places on employers.[5] These arrangements do not, however, preclude voluntary participation if this is permitted by the receiving State, nor do they affect any bilateral or multilateral agreements concerning social security which have been, or may be, concluded between the States in question.

PERSONS BENEFITING FROM PRIVILEGES AND IMMUNITIES

Diplomatic agents

Diplomatic agents, that is to say the head of mission and others of diplomatic rank, have traditionally been granted a degree of immunity which covers both their professional activities and their private acts as individuals—in short, the totality of their existence whilst in the receiving State. This 'global' principle is maintained in the Vienna Convention which provides that diplomatic agents, with the exception of those who are nationals of, or permanently resident

---

[1] Article 35.
[2] Other than members of the family of service staff.
[3] Article 37, paragraphs 1, 2 and 3.　　　　　　　　[4] Article 33.
[5] This requirement does not override the immunity of diplomatic agents from measures of execution. See the statement of the Austrian representative, speaking as chairman of the working party appointed to draft an article relating to social security, *Official Records*, vol. I, p. 193.

in, the receiving State,[1] shall receive the full array of privileges and immunities listed in Articles 29 to 36 relating to personal inviolability, immunity from jurisdiction and fiscal and parafiscal immunities. The question arises as to whether, and if so to what extent, the same benefits should be given to the remaining categories of staff and to other persons connected with the mission. The Vienna Conference, like the International Law Commission before it, experienced considerable difficulty over this issue on which, indeed, more time was spent than on any other provision of the Convention, before a final solution was achieved.

Non-diplomatic members of the staff

As the International Law Commission declared, beyond the undisputed rule that diplomatic members of a mission receive the same privileges and immunities as the head of mission, there is—or was— no uniformity in the practice of States in deciding which members of the staff of a mission should enjoy privileges and immunities.[2] Some States give privileges and immunities on a liberal basis to members of the administrative staff, and a few even to members of the service staff, while others only accord limited rights; certain States make the provision of privileges and immunities dependent on reciprocity, while other States grant none at all. In the absence of any fixed law, the preparation of the Convention required a choice to be made between evaluating the task performed by the subordinate categories of staff as part of the overall operation of the mission, and deciding to what extent privileges and immunities should be accorded on a basis of the function of the particular individual, or group of individuals, concerned. This choice broadly coincided with that between the different forms which any regulation of the matter might take, between a general and uniform rule, founded on what was considered necessary and reasonable from the stand-point of the mission as a whole, and the adoption of minimum provisions, permitting States to make such additional arrangements as they might wish. The solution adopted was largely in accordance with the former approach, whereby the accent was placed on the notion of the mission as an entity, requiring some privileges and immunities for each of its component parts, rather than on a scrupulous application of the test of functional necessity in individual instances.

[1] This qualification extends to all categories. The position of persons who are nationals of, or permanently resident in, the receiving State is considered below, pp. 78–80.
[2] *Yearbook of the International Law Commission, 1958*, vol. II, p. 101.

(a) *Administrative and technical staff*. In the case of administrative and technical staff, there were two counter-tendencies. It was argued, firstly, that persons in this category were in as much need of complete protection as diplomatic agents and should therefore be assimilated to the position of diplomatic agents: they performed important tasks and frequently had access to confidential material—indeed, a cipher clerk might well have possession of more valuable information than a low-ranking diplomat. Furthermore, especially in small missions, it would be very hard to distinguish, according to function, the work of someone of diplomatic rank and that of a member of the administrative and technical staff. As against this it was contended that these considerations, whilst they might be relevant in the case of some administrative and technical staff members, did not apply to all; the number of people involved might be large, perhaps over 5,000 in many capitals,[1] and the persons in the lower categories were, it was said, more prone to abuse their privileges than those of diplomatic rank.

The debate at the Vienna Conference, following long discussions in the Committee of the Whole and in plenary session, finally centred on the extent of the jurisdictional immunity to be accorded to members of the administration and technical staff. The danger that the Conference would adjourn without agreement on this issue was averted by acceptance of a compromise proposal[2] whereby it was agreed that staff members in this category should enjoy the privileges and immunities specified in Articles 29 to 35 'except that the immunity from civil and administrative jurisdiction of the receiving State specified in paragraph 1 of Article 31 shall not extend to acts performed outside the course of their duties'.[3] In addition, in the case of the customs privileges listed in Article 36, these staff members are accorded exemption only in respect of articles imported at the

---

[1] 'Whereas in the past the diplomatic corps in an average capital has numbered 200, there might now be 4,000 on the diplomatic list and four or five times as many subordinate mission staff.' Mr. Bartoš (Yugoslavia), *Yearbook of the International Law Commission, 1957*, vol. I, p. 124.   [2] A/CONF.20/L.21 and Add.2, based on a United Kingdom amendment A/CONF.20/L.20.

[3] Article 37, paragraph 2. See also pp. 64–7 above. Four States, Cambodia, Greece, the United Arab Republic and Venezuela, made reservations regarding this provision when becoming parties to the Convention, and two States, Iraq and Malta, declared it applicable only on a basis of reciprocity. The Federal Republic of Germany stated that it regarded the reservations made by Cambodia and the United Arab Republic (declaring the provision inapplicable), as incompatible with the content and spirit of the Convention. The United Kingdom stated that it did not regard as valid the reservation made by the United Arab Republic.

time of first installation; they do not therefore enjoy any privileges with respect to goods imported subsequently, nor is their personal baggage exempt from inspection.

(b) *Service Staff*. The position of service staff proved easier to settle. Whereas in the case of administrative and technical staff the problem turned on the extent to which they were to be assimilated to diplomatic agents, that issue could not be raised at all with respect to service staff: for them the matter to be determined was which immunities were to be specifically granted. Article 37, paragraph 3, provides that service staff are to be accorded immunity 'in respect of acts performed in the course of their duties', thus leaving them subject, except to that extent, to criminal as well as to civil jurisdiction, to measures of execution and to the obligation to give evidence. They also obtain 'exemption from dues and taxes on the emoluments they receive by reason of their employment' and exemption, subject to the conditions laid down in Article 33, from the social security provisions in force in the receiving State.

Persons connected with members of the staff

(a) *Family members*. The only family members who, by virtue of their relationship, may claim privileges and immunities are those connected with individual members of the first two categories of staff, namely diplomatic agents and administrative and technical personnel. As regards members of the family of a diplomatic agent, there was relatively little disagreement that, in accordance with standard practice, such persons should receive the same privileges and immunities as are accorded to diplomatic agents themselves[1] Except when the family members are nationals of the receiving State, they therefore enjoy the benefits in Articles 29 to 36.

The variations in municipal law regarding such matters as the age when children reach majority and the difficulty in applying the test of economic dependence in all instances prevented the adoption of any precise definition of 'members of the family of a diplomatic agent', other than by the qualification that the persons concerned must form part of the diplomat's household. The International Law Commission stressed, however, that 'close ties or special circumstances'[2] are necessary prerequisites for family relatives wishing to

[1] Article 37, paragraph 1. Even if the diplomatic agent himself does not because he is a national or permanent resident of the receiving State, an anomaly corrected in Article 71, paragraph 2, of the Vienna Convention on Consular Relations.
[2] *Yearbook of the International Law Commission, 1958*, vol. II, p. 102.

claim privileges and immunities. Under Article 10 of the Convention, the ministry of foreign affairs of the receiving State must be notified of the composition of the family and of any changes in it. Although such notification is not conclusive as to the status of the persons concerned, it has an obvious practical utility in enabling the sending State to specify the family members for whom privileges and immunities are sought and in providing the receiving State with an opportunity to query any borderline cases.

Members of the family who form part of the household of a member of the administrative and technical staff receive the same privileges and immunities as the latter, unless they are themselves nationals of, or permanently resident in, the receiving State.[1] Since administrative and technical staff enjoy immunity from civil and administrative jurisdiction only as regards acts performed in the course of their duties, members of their families are accorded no immunity in respect of civil and administrative jurisdiction. Notification must be given to the ministry of foreign affairs of persons claimed as family members.

(b) *Private servants.* Persons in domestic service of members of the mission are granted exemption from taxation on the emoluments they receive by virtue of their employment but are accorded other privileges and immunities 'only to the extent admitted by the receiving State'.[2] That State is required, however, to exercise its jurisdiction so 'as not to interfere unduly with the performance of the functions of the mission'.[3] In accordance with this provision the receiving State would not be entitled to act in such a way as virtually to deprive the staff of a mission of the services of the persons concerned, and should, where possible, notify missions of steps taken, or proposed to be taken, against individual employees which may interrupt their employment.

The private servants of diplomatic agents may be exempt from the social security provisions in force in the receiving State.[4]

Nationals of, or those permanently resident in, the receiving State

(a) *Diplomatic agents.* The appointment as diplomatic agents of

---

[1] Article 37, paragraph 2.　　　　　　　[2] Article 37, paragraph 4.

[3] An adaptation of Article 23 of the Harvard Draft Convention. Harvard Law School, *Research in International Law, I. Diplomatic Privileges and Immunities* (1932), p. 118.

[4] Article 33, paragraph 2. See p. 74 above.

persons having the nationality of the receiving State was strongly opposed during the preparation of the Convention and finally admitted only on the condition that such appointments should be subject to the consent of the receiving State, which may be withdrawn at any time.[1] The question of the extent to which such persons, or those permanently resident in the receiving State, were to be granted privileges and immunities caused a similar battle to be fought, with some fresh complications. In the absence of any clearly established rule on the matter,[2] it was argued that the principle that each State had jurisdiction over its own nationals had priority over the demands of the sending State; accordingly, even if the receiving State agreed to the appointment, it should not be obliged to concede any privileges and immunities to the persons in question. The commoner view, which eventually prevailed, was that, although the receiving State was not bound to consent to the appointment of one of its nationals, if it did so it should accord at least the privileges and immunities which were essential for the execution of official functions. As several representatives stressed, jurisdiction could not in any case be exercised over such agents with respect to acts performed in the course of duty without infringing the sovereign rights of the sending State itself. Article 38 provides that, except where the receiving State agrees to accord additional privileges and immunities, a diplomatic agent who is a national or permanent resident of that State 'shall enjoy only immunity from jurisdiction, and inviolability, in respect of official acts performed in the exercise of his functions'.[3] The Article represents an unsatisfactory compromise in which weight is given to discouraging the appointment of persons other than nationals of the sending State, rather than to the provision of an adequate framework in which non-national diplomatic agents may perform their functions. The fact that the receiving State, in

[1] Article 8, paragraph 2. See pp. 28–9 above. The receiving State may reserve the same right with regard to nationals of a third State who are not also nationals of the sending State (Article 8, paragraph 3), but in this case no qualifications can be placed on the privileges and immunities to be accorded.

[2] *Macartney v. Garbett* (1890) 24 Q.B.D. p. 368, can no longer be regarded as a good authority. See, generally, Satow, *Guide to Diplomatic Practice* (4 ed., 1957), pp. 138–40. Where members of a diplomatic mission of a Commonwealth country and their private servants are citizens both of that Commonwealth country and of the United Kingdom and Colonies, they are accorded the privileges and immunities to which they are entitled under Article 38 as though they are not also citizens of the United Kingdom and Colonies. Similar arrangements exist with respect to Ireland. Diplomatic Privileges (Citizens of the United Kingdom and Colonies) Order, 1964, S.I. 1964, No. 2043.

[3] See p. 64 above. Venezuela made a formal reservation to Article 38.

circumstances where it agrees to the appointment, may agree also to the grant of privileges and immunities on a more regular scale, together with the relatively small number of people involved, prevents the problem from being one of any serious dimensions.

(b) *Other members of the staff and private servants.* In the words of Article 38, paragraph 2, 'Other members of the staff of the mission and private servants who are nationals of or permanently resident in the receiving State shall enjoy privileges and immunities only to the extent admitted by the receiving State.' Having regard to the frequency with which the subordinate grades of mission staff such as chauffeurs, janitors, clerks and interpreters are locally recruited and the dependence of the mission on their services, the sending State may well try to reach agreement with the receiving State that these grades should be treated similarly to their foreign colleagues.

(c) *Family members.* Members of the family of a diplomatic agent are not granted privileges and immunities under the Convention if they are nationals of the receiving State, nor, in the case of members of the family of administrative and technical staff members, if they are either nationals of, or permanently resident in, the receiving State.[1]

DURATION OF PRIVILEGES AND IMMUNITIES

The temporal extent of the privileges and immunities which may be claimed by an individual depends, in the case of a member of the staff of a mission, on the duration of his functions, and, as regards persons whose entitlement is derivative, namely family members and private servants, on the duration of the relationship. This general statement is subject to certain qualifications, which are considered below.

From what moment may privileges and immunities be claimed?

Paragraph 1 of Article 39 distinguishes between persons outside and those inside the receiving State at the time of appointment. A person who is outside the country is entitled to privileges and immunities 'from the moment he enters the territory of the receiving State on proceeding to take up his post'; in the case of a person already in the receiving State, his enjoyment of privileges and immunities begins

[1] Article 37, paragraphs 1 and 2.

80

'from the moment when his appointment is notified to the Ministry of Foreign Affairs' or other appropriate ministry. The question of the moment in time when privileges and immunities are to be accorded by the receiving State is thus distinguished from, and not made dependent on, the consent of that State to the appointment as such. Except in the case of the head of mission, service attachés and its own nationals, the receiving State cannot countermand the choice of personnel made by the sending State and, subject to such control as it may exert under the provisions of Article 10 or as regards the grant of an entry visa, is accordingly obliged to grant the requisite privileges and immunities to any persons appointed.[1] In the case of family members and private servants the enjoyment of privileges and immunities is dependent on the nature of the relationship; appropriate notification must be given to the foreign ministry.[2]

A certain retroactive effect is gained in the sphere of jurisdictional immunity as regards actions involving facts or legal situations created before the appointment was made; the essential factor is that the agent should be invested with an official character at the time when the action is brought or before it is concluded.[3] A matter of some obscurity, however, concerns the effect upon the plaintiff's rights in cases which are halted in this way: are they annihilated or merely suspended? Where the diplomat is already at his post at the time when the action is initiated, the answer is debatable; writs and processes falling under the Act of Anne were declared null and void, but the effect of any waiver was to render them voidable.[4] Where the member of the mission was not yet appointed, or not yet appointed at a sufficient level, when the writ was issued, the argument for holding that the plaintiff's rights are merely suspended for the period of the defendant's privileged status is so much the stronger, as a United States court held in the case of *Arcaya v. Paez*,[5] a view which received some support in the English Court of Appeal in the case of *Ghosh v. D'Rozario.*[6]

---

[1] See p. 25 above. Several States reserved their position in view of the wording of Article 39 and declared that, in accordance with their prevailing practice, they would continue to require that all persons be both notified to and accepted by them, before privileges and immunities were accorded. See the statements made by the representatives of Switzerland, United States and Italy, *Official Records*, vol. I, pp. 209 and 37.

[2] Article 10, paragraph 1(*b*), (*c*) and (*d*).

[3] *Procureur général c. Nazare Aga*, Kiss, *Répertoire de la pratique française en matière de droit international public* (1965), tome III, no. 578, pp. 330–1.

[4] See p. 64 above.   [5] *International Law Reports*, 1956, p. 436.

[6] [1962] 2 All E.R. p. 640, at p. 646 (Davies L.J.).

The later case of *Empson v. Smith*,[1] although dependent on the particular facts of its timing, provides a neat balance to *Arcaya v. Paez* and *Ghosh v. D'Rozario*. In 1963 Mr. Smith, an administrative officer employed at the Canadian High Commission in London, pleaded immunity and obtained a stay of proceedings brought against him for breach of a tenancy agreement. While the decision was in the course of appeal the Diplomatic Privileges Act, 1964, was adopted, Article 37, paragraph 2, of which limits the immunity from civil proceedings of members of the administrative staff to acts performed in the course of their functions. The Court of Appeal upheld the appeal of Mrs. Empson on the ground that the initial action was voidable, not void, and, since the Act itself was of a procedural nature, it should be applied retrospectively to remove the bar to her claim. Although the characterization of the Act as a procedural statute may be queried,[2] the fact that immunity could not be claimed for an action on the same facts commenced at the present time lends support to the rationale of the judgement.

At what moment do privileges and immunities end?
The answer to this question is more complex. In the usual case privileges and immunities cease when the functions of the member of the mission staff concerned come to an end and he leaves the country. The staff member is, however, given a 'reasonable period' in which to arrange his affairs after his functions have ended, and it is only if he fails to depart after its expiry that action may be brought against him.[3] The answers to the question of what constitutes a 'reasonable period' depends on the circumstances; in the event of an armed conflict or if the affairs of the mission itself have to be wound up, it may well be an appreciable length of time. Frequently the two States will agree between themselves on the details and it is only exceptionally (though it is those exceptions which are recorded in the books) that the matter falls to be determined by the courts. In some instances the sending State may itself facilitate the exercise of local jurisdiction by terminating the functions of the employee and waiving his immunity. In 1940 a coding clerk at the United States Embassy in

---

[1] [1965] 2 All E.R. 881.

[2] See the case note by P. Jackson, *Modern Law Review*, 28 (1965), p. 710.

[3] Article 39, paragraph 2. The leading case is *Magdalena Steam Navigation Company v. Martin* (1859) 2 E. and E. p. 94; on the English authorities see Jones, 'Termination of Diplomatic Immunity', *British Year Book of International Law*, xxv (1948), p. 262. See, generally, Salmon, 'Les limites dans le temps de l'immunité de juridiction des agents diplomatiques', *Travaux et Conférences*, tome x, p. 37.

London was caught engaging in espionage activities. He was instantly discharged and his immunity waived. The Court of Criminal Appeal rejected the argument presented on his behalf, that he was entitled to diplomatic immunity for a reasonable period after the end of his employment sufficient to enable him to make arrangements to leave the country freely.[1]

The other major qualification concerns acts performed 'in the exercise of his functions' by a person entitled to privileges and immunities. In this case the immunity 'shall continue to subsist', in recognition of the fact that the acts in question represent, in a direct sense, that of the sending State itself and not those which the member of the mission has performed in a personal capacity.[2]

In the case of the death of a member of the mission, the members of his family continue to enjoy 'the privileges and immunities to which they are entitled until the expiry of a reasonable period in which to leave the country'.[3] The movable property of the deceased[4] may be removed, with the exception of any property acquired in the receiving State the export of which is prohibited.

NON-DISCRIMINATION AND RECIPROCITY

The rules laid down in the Vienna Convention, like the customary rules they are intended to supplant, are designed to be of general application. In principle, therefore, they should be applied in a uniform manner to all the States concerned. The fact that the Convention provides for the establishment of what are essentially bilateral relationships prevents the principle of non-discrimination from being taken as the sole determinant however; the operation of the principle is qualified by that of the principle of reciprocity, which places the accent on the autonomy of the particular States involved. Despite the familiarity of this fact, the relationship between the two principles concerned is not one which can be easily reduced to simple terms. Moreover, as became clear during the discussions in the International Law Commission, different shades of meaning may be attributed to the two notions. Does 'non-discrimination' mean that

[1] *R v. Kent* [1941] 1 K.B. p. 454. See also *Re Suarez* [1918] 1 Ch. 176.
[2] See p. 64 above.   [3] Article 39, paragraph 3.
[4] Whether a member of the mission staff or of the family of a member of the staff. It may be noted that diplomatic privileges and immunities 'preclude a coroner from investigating the death of a person who, if alive, would have been entitled to diplomatic immunity unless the privilege is waived'. *Jervis on the Office and Duties of Coroners* (9 ed., 1957), p. 22, quoted in Lyons, op cit., *British Year Book of International Law*, xxxiv (1958), p. 372.

X, a receiving State, is to provide the same treatment to the mission it receives from State A as it does to the mission from State B? Or is the comparison to be made between the treatment given to the missions which are exchanged by a pair of States so that if one State deviates from the standard the other may do likewise? As regards the principle of reciprocity, does this mean no more than the positive form of non-discrimination—that State X should grant the same rights to the mission of State A as A grants to the mission of X—or is it only properly invoked where the two States are prepared to accord each other advantages over and above the minimum internationally prescribed? What action may be taken by sending States when the rules are applied by a given receiving State, not more liberally but more restrictively than is the norm, or more restrictively than the sending State is itself providing in its capacity as a receiving State?

The International Law Commission considered these issues at length before adopting as the initial, and more basic, principle, that, 'the receiving State shall not discriminate as between States'[1] when applying the rules laid down in the Convention. Receiving States are therefore under an obligation to provide uniform treatment to all missions they have agreed to receive. This general rule is set aside in two sets of circumstances in which, although unequal treatment is implied, no discrimination is deemed to occur since the action in question is based on the principle of reciprocity. The first of these instances is that in which a receiving State applies any of the provisions of the Convention restrictively because of a restrictive interpretation of the same provision to its mission in the sending State.[2] In its commentary the International Law Commission distinguished between an interpretation which, though restrictive, is in keeping with the terms of the rule, and one amounting to an infringement of the rule; action taken by the receiving State in the latter instance constitutes an act of reprisal and not one founded on reciprocity.[3]

It is not hard to imagine that disputes may well occur as to whether or not a given action is merely restrictive or constitutes a breach of the obligation concerned. More generally, the question may be raised which provisions of the Convention can in fact be restrictively interpreted without infringing the duty imposed on the receiving State? Although many of the articles are cast in wide terms, some at least must be regarded as peremptory norms. In the case of

[1] Article 47, paragraph 1.   [2] Article 47, paragraph 2(a).
[3] *Yearbook of the International Law Commission, 1958*, vol. II, p. 105.

the personal inviolability of diplomatic agents and the inviolability of missions, to take the most extreme examples, it is difficult to see how the obligation imposed on the receiving State could be restrictively applied (except, possibly, by agreement) without infliction of an international wrong. At the least the rules concerned must be those in which a certain latitude is left to States in the formulation used. It is of interest to note that when, in 1955, the British Government adopted legislation to enable it to withdraw the privileges and immunities enjoyed by specified classes of persons attached to diplomatic missions in London, so as to place the persons concerned in a position corresponding as closely as possible to that of persons connected with certain British missions abroad, the immunities withdrawn were 'immunity from suit or legal process (*except* in respect of things done or omitted to be done in the course of the performance of official duties) and inviolability of residence'.[1] By Orders in Council made in accordance with this provision the immunity of subordinate classes of officials and of private servants of a number of diplomatic missions were curtailed; the immunity from suit or legal process of members of the families of the officials concerned was removed entirely.[2] Section 3(1) of the Diplomatic Privileges Act, 1964, contains a similar power, cast in wider terms, enabling the United Kingdom Government to withdraw privileges and immunities either from the foreign mission itself or from persons connected with it, where those accorded to the United Kingdom mission or its personnel in the country in question are less than those presently being accorded in London.

The other major instance in which the principle of non-discrimination is inapplicable occurs 'where by custom or agreement States extend to each other more favourable treatment than is required by the provisions' of the Convention.[3] In this circumstance it is only natural, as was said by the International Law Commission, that

[1] Section 3(1), Diplomatic Immunities Restriction Act, 1955, now repealed by the Diplomatic Privileges Act, 1964 (Italics added). *N.B.* The 1955 Act was an enabling statute only from the standpoint of United Kingdom law; it did not constitute a unilateral creation of rights not previously existing under international law.

[2] The restrictions imposed by the Diplomatic Immunities Restriction Act, 1955, and the accompanying Orders in Council (Diplomatic Immunities Restriction Order, 1956, S.I. 1956, No. 84) were subsequently modified by agreement with Bulgaria, Czechoslovakia, Hungary and the USSR, in exchange for an improvement in the position of persons attached to the British Embassies in those countries. See p. 86 below and, as regards the personnel of the USSR Embassy, S.I. 1956, No. 1579.

[3] Article 47, paragraph 2(*b*).

States should be free to make the grant of benefits in excess of the obligatory minimum conditional on receiving equal treatment in return.[1] As regards the situation in the United Kingdom, Section 7(1) of the 1964 Act declares that, where any agreement between any State and the United Kingdom at the time when the Act came into force provides for extending

(*a*) such immunity from jurisdiction and from arrest or detention, and such inviolability of residence, as are conferred by this Act on a diplomatic agent, or

(*b*) such exemption from customs duties, taxes and related charges as is conferred by this Act in respect of articles for the personal use of a diplomatic agent;

to any class of person, or to articles for the personal use of any class of person, connected with the mission of that State, that immunity and inviolability or exemption shall so extend, so long as that agreement or arrangement continues in force.

As was explained in the House of Commons, this provision was included to enable persons (chiefly subordinate staff) connected with British missions in certain countries to receive, in the first case, more extensive protection than is provided under the Convention and, in the second case, more extensive privileges. The pertinent agreements in the first category were negotiated after the adoption of the Diplomatic Immunities Restriction Act, 1955, and the accompanying statutory instruments, when it was agreed with four East European countries[2] that the United Kingdom would restore to members of the non-diplomatic staff and to servants employed at the London Embassy the immunity from suit and legal process which had been withdrawn, provided members of the British Embassy concerned below the rank of attaché, their families, embassy servants and personal servants of the Ambassador (excluding local nationals) were granted similar immunities.[3] Section 7(1)(*a*) of the Diplomatic

---

[1] *Yearbook of the International Law Commission, 1958*, vol. II, p. 105.

[2] The notes exchanged with the USSR are reproduced in *British Practice in International Law, 1964—II* (ed. Lauterpacht), pp. 226–8.

[3] In the case of the USSR the United Kingdom found it necessary to ask that the persons concerned at the British Embassy in Moscow should be accorded 'immunity from personal arrest or other legal process and from the civil and criminal jurisdiction of the Soviet courts and inviolability of residence'. Thus, though the final result was to enable the two groups to enjoy an equal position, the United Kingdom personnel moved from a position which was inferior to that which their USSR counterparts enjoyed, even after the issue of the Diplomatic Immunities Restriction Order, 1956, S.I. 1956, No. 84. The statement of the Minister of State for Foreign Affairs that 'we feel that we get as much advantage from (the reciprocal agreement of 1956) as the Soviet Union does', is accordingly substantiated, despite the fact that, in 1964, the United Kingdom accorded the

Privileges Act, 1964, was therefore drafted so to enable these arrangements to continue; members of the administrative and technical
staff, service staff and private servants employed at the Bulgarian,
Czech, Hungarian and USSR Embassies in London receive the
benefits derived from that paragraph, as do their opposite members
in the United Kingdom missions to those countries.[1] The additional
privileges referred to in Section 7(1)(*b*) are given to the members of
the administrative and technical staff of the missions of nine countries, in return for equal treatment to British staff of the same category serving in the States concerned.[2]

TRANSIT THROUGH THIRD STATES

The *corpus* of the Vienna Convention is concerned with the regulation of diplomatic representation between pairs of States, in their
individual capacities as sending and receiving States. Third States fall
outside this bilateral pattern, although plainly diplomatic missions
could not be maintained unless the personnel connected with them
were allowed to pass through such States on their way to and from
their posts. Although a customary rule existed—and exists still—
governing the action of third States, its ambit and requirements
were vague. Moreover no immediate basis of reciprocity under-
writes the attitude of third States, nor is the test of functional necessity directly applicable in their regard. The International Law
Commission and the Vienna Conference sought, therefore, not so
much to consolidate existing practices as to determine the extremes
within which States sending diplomats and those according them
transit may henceforth operate. The issues can be reduced to two:
whether third States are bound to allow mission staff to pass through
their territories, and, if such persons do travel through third States,
what privileges and immunities are to be granted them.

The International Law Commission declined to deal explicitly
with the first question; some members declared firmly that transit
States, as part of the community of nations, were bound to accord

---

additional privileges in question to a total of 161 individuals and 80 wives, from
four East European countries, as opposed to 128 United Kingdom citizens and
61 wives stationed in those countries; the difference in numbers is chiefly due to
the employment by the East European countries of their own nationals as
chauffeurs. See *British Practice in International Law, 1964—II* (ed. Lauterpacht),
pp. 224–5.

[1] *London Gazette*, Note No. 43451, 2 October 1964. Ibid., pp. 225–6.

[2] Idem. The countries concerned are Belgium, Bulgaria, France, Germany,
Indonesia, Luxembourg, Netherlands, Poland and the United States.

passage to the diplomats of other Governments, even if they did not recognize the particular Government concerned; others, equally firmly, argued that transit States had the final right to decide who should be admitted to their territories. Since the Commission had previously determined that receiving States should not be placed under an obligation to admit persons appointed to serve with a mission, it was difficult to provide that third States should be subject to a more stringent rule. Noting, somewhat weakly it may be thought, that the problem only arises rarely, the Commission did not think it necessary to proceed further.[1] Although no declaration of principle was introduced, the question of the right of passage was touched on twice at the Conference. Firstly, the transit of a diplomatic agent and others connected with a mission is made conditional, if the third State so chooses, on the grant of a passport visa;[2] a third State can accordingly take steps to ensure that foreign mission staff do not pass through its territory without its consent. Secondly, transit States are obliged to grant the same treatment to persons, and to official communications and diplomatic bags, whose presence in the transit State is due to *force majeure* as they are to those whose presence is optional;[3] by parity of reasoning therefore, a third State is not otherwise obliged to accord such treatment unless it has agreed to allow the persons or objects concerned to cross its territory.

Turning to the standard of treatment to be granted to those whose transit is recognized under the Convention, the position varies according to the category of person involved. A diplomatic agent travelling to take up or to return to his post, or when returning to his own country,[4] is accorded 'inviolability and such other immunities as may be required to ensure his transit or return'. What these 'other immunities' are is not further specified but include immunity from criminal jurisdiction and, perhaps, immunity from civil jurisdiction.[5]

[1] *Yearbook of the International Law Commission, 1958*, vol. I, p. 103.

[2] Article 40.

[3] Article 40, paragraph 4. A more common occurrence than it was, owing to the diversion of planes caused, for example, by bad weather conditions.

[4] When the representative is travelling to or from an international conference or a meeting of an international organization a conventional instrument may apply, as well as the customary rule embodied in Article 40. It was in this sense that Article 40 was invoked in the course of the Ivory Coast–Guinea dispute in 1967. See S/8120, annex XII, 14 August 1967, and p. 123 below.

[5] The International Law Commission did not reach a definite conclusion on the point. *Yearbook of the International Law Commission, 1957*, vol. I, pp. 91–2, and *Yearbook of the International Law Commission, 1958*, vol. I, pp. 173–4. Practice provides no clear guidance as to the extent of jurisdictional immunity, though see *Bergman v. De Sieyès, Annual Digest*, 1947, p. 150.

The same privileges and immunities are extended to members of the family of a diplomatic agent. In the case of members of other categories of staff and their families, third States are merely placed under an obligation not to hinder their transit.[1] Lastly, in the case of official communications, diplomatic couriers (who may be required to obtain a passport visa), and diplomatic bags, the sending State may claim on their behalf the same treatment from the transit State as the receiving State itself is bound to accord.[2]

SPECIAL MISSIONS

The Vienna Convention on Diplomatic Relations deals only with permanent diplomatic representation between States; it does not cover the two other forms of representation which are to be discussed, the use of special missions, or *ad hoc* diplomacy as it is often called, and representation at international organizations. The dispatch of special missions constitutes in fact the earliest of all forms of diplomatic relations, preceding the custom of exchanging permanent embassies and envoys. With the growth of the latter practice from the seventeenth and eighteenth centuries on, special missions fell into disuse; up until a short time ago they were sent almost exclusively in order to represent the sending State or its ruling family on ceremonial occasions—at coronations, presidential installations, royal weddings and so forth. Indeed it is virtually only in this context that Satow[3] refers to them. As a relatively rare and limited phenomenon, they received little attention in the books and no clear rules of practice emerged to regulate their status. The sources of law were scanty and unreliable and there was no settled answer to the question whether, and if so to what extent, members of the staff of such missions enjoyed privileges and immunities comparable to those given to embassy or consular staff. So long as privileges were accorded no problem arose, but if they were refused or withdrawn for any reason, the first question posed was the fundamental one: on what basis does the representative concerned have a right to special treatment?

This has remained the position even though special missions have been used by States to an ever increasing extent over the past twenty years, in almost every field of official business. Three main reasons

[1] Article 40, paragraph 2. There is, in addition, the duty of protection owed to all persons within their territory.
[2] Article 40, paragraph 3.
[3] Satow, op. cit. (4 ed., 1957), pp. 40–2, 115, 151, 207, 274.

account for this development: the availability of rapid air transport; the increase in state activity in all spheres, which has placed the accent on political direction—the attempt, in short, to do more, about more things, which has led the political leaders and interested officials of different countries to meet more frequently; and, lastly, the need for regulation of matters requiring technical expertise. As regards the first cause there is little that I need to add: the airline timetables are known to all. Mr. Dulles, when Secretary of State, flew some 23,000 miles a year; Lord Chalfont averaged 100,000 and Mr. Hasluck, the Australian Foreign Minister, gave his annual figure as well over that.[1] The politicalization of public and international law similarly requires little embroidery. Policy-makers have become in a very real sense their own diplomats, whether in the search for agreement with ideological opponents or in the conduct of regional and military alliances. Whilst permanent envoys and missions retain their importance, it is no longer an exclusive importance; increasingly they are adjuncts (particularly, ironically enough, in the larger capitals) to a complex process in which the chief roles are played by the various ministers and others who are able to fly in for a discussion with the corresponding member of the administration of the receiving State, or to attend a meeting organized within the framework of the various inter-governmental bodies. The main task of the professional diplomat often consists not so much of independent policy appreciation and negotiation as of 'follow-up' or 'support' action—establishing contact with the local press and other mass media, maintaining public relations, and preparing for forthcoming sessions of the major international organizations.

Besides missions at ministerial level, there are two other categories which may be broadly distinguished. The first consists of what are sometimes termed 'standard' missions, namely missions, often composed of senior governmental officials, which are sent to deal with topics falling within the scope of official business and requiring co-operation between the States concerned; some of the commonest topics for such missions are matters relating to trade and financial affairs, defence arrangements, scientific and cultural activities and questions relating to communications. While a certain proportion of these missions may have political implications, others—for example, regarding the co-ordination of national railways or plans for joint hydroelectric development—may be of a more limited nature. Missions of the latter sort may therefore fall in the remaining category of

[1] *The Times*, 11 October 1966, p. 11, cols. 6–7.

so-called 'low-level' missions, consisting of missions sent to discuss questions of purely technical or administrative significance, although it is often difficult to draw a precise line between the two classes. Since external relations are no longer solely, even though they remain primarily, a matter of concern to foreign ministries, the various home departments and major public corporations may thus each be engaged, in varying degrees, with the conduct of a 'foreign policy' with their counterparts abroad.

Although States have used the device of sending a special mission increasingly, no definite rules have emerged to prescribe the conditions under which such missions may be sent and received. If we were prepared to wait long enough presumably rules might be created by custom—but that would be a long process and, having regard to the varied character of these missions, it is in any case doubtful how effective a solution this would be. The International Law Commission accordingly sought to deal with the matter by producing an agreed text, similar to the process used in the case of diplomatic and consular relations. In 1967 the Commission adopted a series of final draft articles and a commentary, based on the reports of its Special Rapporteur (Mr. M. Bartoš (Yugoslavia)), the comments made by Governments and the views expressed in the United Nations Sixth Committee. These draft articles were submitted to the General Assembly at its twenty-second session with a recommendation that appropriate steps should be taken for the conclusion of a Convention.[1] Following consideration by the Sixth Committee the General Assembly decided that the item should be placed on the agenda of its twenty-third session, with a view to the adoption of a Convention on Special Missions by the Assembly itself. Although a definitive set of provisions accordingly still needs to be adopted by States, the steps already taken, in particular the recommendation by the International Law Commission of a set of final draft articles and the

---

[1] *Report of the International Law Commission on the work of its nineteenth session, 1967, General Assembly Official Records: Twenty-second session, Suppl. No. 9* (A/6709/Rev.1) (subsequently referred to as '*1967 ILC Report*') Mr. Bartoš submitted reports in 1964 (*Yearbook of the International Law Commission, 1964*, vol. II, p. 67), 1965 (*Yearbook of the International Law Commission, 1965*, vol. II, p. 109), 1966 (A/CN.4/189 and Add.1 and 2) and 1967 (A/CN.4/194, and Add.1–5). The draft articles adopted by the Commission in 1964 and 1965 were considerably modified in 1967.

The history of earlier United Nations examination of the subject (including brief consideration at the Vienna Conference on Diplomatic Relations) is summarized in a Secretariat working paper, *Yearbook of the International Law Commission, 1963*, vol. II, p. 154.

discussions held, provide a basis on which to distinguish the main problems involved and the likely outcome.

The most basic issue confronting the Commission, as the initial codifying agent, was that of deciding whether an attempt should be made to regulate the legal status of all the entities which might claim to be special missions, or whether some only should be selected. If the first approach was followed it would be necessary to specify the precise distinction between the main categories, namely 'high-level', 'standard' and 'low-level' missions, and, having made this differentiation, to provide separate legal rules for each category. Since it became evident that Governments would require a high degree of flexibility in any scheme put forward, the result of following this approach was likely to be an extremely complicated instrument, and one which, if only for that reason, might be often bypassed in practice. The crucial problem for the Commission thus became that of finding a suitable criterion by which to differentiate those missions which could be brought within the framework of a single, uniform treaty, and those others, of relatively less importance, which might be considered merely as visits made under official auspices. The solution eventually chosen by the Commission was to decide that the proposed draft articles should deal solely with special missions having a representative character, that is to say, with missions which might be regarded as organs of the sending State and as having the legal capacity to express the will of that State within the limits of their specified task. Persons who represent only part of the State—for example members of public bodies or party delegations—are therefore excluded, as are the so-called 'low-level' missions. To ensure that the representative element is present, the Commission specified that each mission must contain at least one person who has been designated as a 'representative of the sending State in the special mission'.[1] To complete the definition, besides its representative character a special mission must be of a temporary character (even if not necessarily very short), as opposed to an embassy which is intended to be of indefinite duration, and, lastly, the mission must have a specific task—it does not have a general representative capacity such as a normal diplomatic mission possesses.[2]

---

[1] Articles l(e) and 9, *1967 ILC Report*. It may be noted that the composition of a special mission may include members of a permanent diplomatic mission, who retain their privileges and immunities as members of such missions.

[2] A problem may arise in practice, however, if the mission includes someone of foreign minister rank or above who has, by virtue of his position, a general representative capacity.

As regards the conditions under which a special mission may be sent, the most important, as in the case of permanent missions, is that both States must give their consent; in this instance, however, not only must the receiving State agree to the dispatch of the special mission, but the task to be performed is also subject to mutual agreement. The way in which consent to the sending of a mission is given is often more informal than in the case of permanent institutions; frequently a note or a letter is sent from the embassy of the sending State to the foreign ministry of the receiving State, but consent may also be assumed, perhaps following a conversation with the official of the host State directly concerned. In the case of agreement over the mission's function, it may be similarly difficult on occasions to discover at what moment and to what degree consent has been given, particularly if the task is of a general character (for example, to sound out the political attitude of the other Government), or if the task changes or evolves during discussions, but the element of consent remains essential. An important distinction from permanent missions, however, is that mutual recognition of the two countries is not a prerequisite —although the dispatch of a special mission may, in practice, often serve as a prelude to such a step. Nor, although this follows naturally from the above, are diplomatic and consular relations an essential precondition, but in their absence the special mission will not, of course, be able to use the existing facilities, from desk space to couriers, which permanent installations can provide. Similarly as regards the termination of a special mission, the outbreak of armed conflict or the severance of diplomatic relations will not necessarily mean the ending of a special mission. The absence of reciprocity provides a further point of differentiation; there is usually no question of an exchange of special missions as such but simply the one-way dispatch of a mission from the sending State to the receiving State— even though the performance of the mission's task frequently requires, in effect, the appointment of a 'mission' composed of officials of equivalent rank on the part of the receiving State also (the 'home team' as it were). As an alternative arrangement, indicative of the flexible nature of the institution, special missions may, however, be sent by two States to meet on the territory of a third, subject to the latter's consent.[1]

The major remaining issue concerns the privileges and immunities

---

[1] Article 18, *1967 ILC Report*. The third State retains the right to withdraw its consent at any time and may make its consent subject to such conditions as it may see fit.

of special missions. To what extent are they to be treated as analogous to permanent missions and to what extent are they to be given a distinct position of their own? In answering this question the International Law Commission was guided by its previous decision to deal solely with special missions of a representative character. The Commission therefore decided to adopt a single set of provisions applicable to all missions[1] based as closely as possible on the language of the Vienna Convention on Diplomatic Relations, but allowing for their particular character and functions; objections have been raised, however, that this represents too liberal a starting point. Of central importance to the operation of the proposed Convention is the fact that there is nothing to prevent the two States from agreeing that a particular mission shall have a status smaller or greater than that laid down as a general standard, i.e. the future Convention is a code of provisions which States may choose to follow rather than an obligatory set of rules: *ius dispositivum* rather than *ius cogens*. As a technique of codifying the law the proposed Convention is one of somewhat more sophistication than perhaps appears at first sight. In the case of diplomatic missions the major provision of the Vienna Convention becomes applicable once the initial steps have been taken and the extent to which States may deviate from the provisions is subject to the restrictions regarding non-discrimination and reciprocity.[2] The situation with respect to special missions is different: the attempt here is to set out a body of rules more closely resembling a standard form of contract, with a right for the parties to agree to vary its terms at will. It should not be concluded that this is an ineffectual solution to the problems posed in providing a legal framework to govern the status of special missions. These missions, even within the limitations set by the International Law Commission, are sent for many purposes and may contain a variety of persons; there is no reason to apply a rigid pattern to them. The existence of an authoritative group of articles which may form the basis for individual agreements thus fills the gap in the previous arsenal of state practice and enables Governments to maintain their diplomatic contacts through special missions in a way that adequately combines both freedom and security.

---

[1] When missions include persons of high rank, e.g. a head of State or a foreign minister, these persons retain the facilities, privileges and immunities conferred on them by international law, but the mission itself receives no special status. Article 21, *1967 ILC Report*.

[2] See p. 83 above. Article 50, *1967 ILC Report*, lays down the principle of non-discrimination in respect of special missions also, but allows exceptions to the extent stated above.

Chapter V

REPRESENTATION AT
INTERNATIONAL ORGANIZATIONS

INTRODUCTION

WHEREAS diplomacy was formerly concerned chiefly with relations between individual States, with the development of international organizations it has become multilateral in form and collective in its aspirations, based furthermore on a series of agreements which give the international organization itself a distinct and independent status. This is not to say that the original pattern of diplomacy has been dissolved—as we have seen the relevant legal rules have recently been redefined so as to enable this form of diplomacy to maintain its effectiveness. But the bilateral machinery has become only a segment of the whole, its role distorted unless the complete framework is kept in view. In describing the legal position of diplomatic missions and agents it is also necessary therefore to describe the complex situation which results when a major organization is established, without territorial jurisdiction of its own,[1] and composed of member States each of which is entitled to representation at its headquarters. This is the position with respect to the United Nations, the specialized agencies, the principal regional bodies—the Arab League, the Council of Europe, the Organization of African Unity and the Organization of American States—and the important economic institutions on our own continent, the European Economic Community, the European Coal and Steel Community and Euratom.

In many particulars the practices followed are the same as,

[1] States now acting as hosts to the permanent offices of major international organizations include the following: Austria (IAEA), Belgium (EEC and Euratom), Canada (ICAO), Chile (Economic Commission for Latin America), Ethiopia (Economic Commission for Africa and Organization of African Unity), France (Council of Europe and UNESCO), Italy (FAO), Luxembourg (ECSC), Netherlands (International Court of Justice), Switzerland (ILO, ITU, United Nations, UPU, WHO, WMO), Thailand (Economic Commission for Asia and the Far East), United Arab Republic (Arab League), USSR (COMECON), United Kingdom (IMCO) and United States (IBRD, IDA, IFC, IMF, Organization of American States and United Nations).

or similar to, those accorded to diplomatic missions and agents There is, however, a distinctive feature in this instance, namely, the presence of the international organization itself, at once a subject of international law in its own right and an entity made up of States that are its members. The organization does not grant recognition to its members, important though membership may be in determining the attitude of States in their individual relations, nor does it normally exchange missions with them; nor, lastly, can it supply a complete system of municipal law, such as national States can provide. Nevertheless it represents the fundamental reason for the presence of the diplomats concerned and the focal point of their activities. Not only, therefore, must the internal rules of these organizations be examined in order to see to what extent state representatives cease to act as individual envoys and acquire international (or extra-national) characteristics and responsibilities—a series of factors which do not occur in bilateral diplomatic relations—it is also necessary to consider the various issues which arise from the standpoint of the organization itself, which has an interest of its own in ensuring that official representatives are able to attend meetings and exercise their functions freely. The position of the host State, honourable, and indeed, politically valuable though it may be, is a delicate and difficult one. It must be prepared to accept the presence of a potentially large number of persons from countries with which it may maintain no, or at best, guarded, relations, and to accord to the delegates concerned at least the most essential privileges and immunities. The precise delimitation of the powers of the host State, of the rights of the individual member States, and of the organization as a whole, is accordingly an intricate affair, involving the examination of a number of international instruments.

I shall not deal with all the questions which may arise or with their detailed resolution, but only with the major features of the practice which has emerged, in particular with those aspects which differentiate this practice from that observed in bilateral diplomatic relations. I shall concentrate on the position at the United Nations and at the European organizations at Brussels since the procedures evolved at these institutions are, in their several ways, the most developed and influential.

In principle the delegates sent by Governments to international organizations represent, by definition, the State which appointed them, and execute functions which have much in common with those performed at international conferences and by diplomatic missions:[1] the safeguarding and advancing of national interests through negotiation, discussion and observation, in accordance with official instructions. Nevertheless the task on which they are engaged cannot be identified with the immediate execution of national policies; the realization of the objectives of the organization requires that consideration be given to the interests of the whole. Even if States should sometimes fall short of that ideal, the mechanics of the organization enforce collective action and, on occasions, collective representation. Thus, whether regarded in terms of the entity which delegates represent or the function they perform, there is often a mingling of national and international elements to be considered. While the entire field cannot be exhaustively studied here, the following survey distinguishes some of the main forms of state representation at international organizations.

Representation within the organization

(a) *Choice of representation in plenary bodies.* Although each member State is normally free to select the individuals who are to represent it in a given plenary body, the criteria which are to guide its choice may be carefully prescribed as a means of advancing the objectives of the organization. Besides technical institutions, such as the Universal Postal Union and the World Meteorological Organization, where expert knowledge on the part of delegates is an obvious prerequisite, provision may be made for the representation of interests which are neither highly specialized nor coincident with government functions. In the case of the International Labour Organization for example, the delegation of a Member State to the General Conference is made up of a workers' and an employers' delegate, chosen in agreement with the bodies representing those two groups in the country in question, as well as two delegates, usually from the ministry of labour or similar department, chosen by

---

[1] Representatives at international organizations, unless also accredited to the host State, do not, however, have the task of protecting the interests of their fellow nationals in that State or of collecting information regarding local conditions.

the executive.[1] In other instances the constituent instrument may deliberately attempt to secure national representation at a specified level, so as to ensure that the work of the organization receives the necessary degree of official attention and co-operation. Thus, most regional organizations include an organ on which the representative must be a member of the Government of the member State, normally the foreign minister.

(*b*) *Representation in restricted organs.* Besides rules of this kind, uniformly applicable to all member States, representation in a limited body within the organization may also be made subject to qualifications which emphasize the international or trans-national interest involved. Apart from organs such as the Security Council in which, although decisions are taken on behalf of the whole Organization, delegates are chosen exclusively by individual Governments,[2] in others, while the element of national representation remains, official regard is paid to the individual qualities of the particular persons selected. The Executive Board of the World Health Organization, for example, consists of technically qualified members designated by the States which have themselves been elected by the Health Assembly.[3] At one stage further on, the individuals may themselves be chosen directly by a collective process: the Governing Body of the International Labour Organization is composed in part of workers' and employers' delegates elected by their respective fellow-delegates to the General Conference;[4] and the Executive Board of UNESCO is made up entirely of individuals elected by the General Conference from among the delegates sent by Member States.[5] Whereas, therefore, representatives serving on the Security Council have a double function, acting both on behalf of the State which sends them and on behalf of the international community, an individual elected to the executive organ of the International Labour Organization or of UNESCO is called upon more directly to serve in an international capacity, and it is to the Organization that he

[1] Article 3, ILO Constitution. Furthermore the Conference may 'refuse to admit any delegate or adviser whom it deems not to have been nominated in accordance with this Article'. Idem.

[2] Article 23 of the Charter. Under Article 24 Member States agree that, in carrying out its primary responsibility for the maintenance of international peace and security 'the Security Council acts on their behalf'.

[3] Article 24, WHO Constitution.

[4] Article 7, ILO Constitution.

[5] Article v, UNESCO Constitution.

must look for the protection of the privileges and immunities which he needs in order to perform his functions.[1]

(c) *Fusion of national and international functions.* Although in the case of the executive bodies of the International Labour Organizations, UNESCO and the World Health Organization, the demands of international representation are given some degree of precedence over those of purely national representation, in other instances state and organizational functions may tend to merge with one another. Besides the case of the Security Council, which has just been noted, the most striking illustration of this phenomenon is provided by the Executive Directors of the International Bank. Five of these are appointed by the five States having the largest number of shares in the Bank, the remaining fifteen being elected by the Board of Governors.[2] The Executive Directors hold regular meetings throughout the year and conduct, together with the President, the current affairs of the Bank. They have their offices in the building of the International Bank, are paid by the Bank in recognition of their services, and are regularly reported to Member States and to the Secretary-General as entitled to privileges and immunities *qua* 'functionnaires' of the Bank, under the Convention on the Privileges and Immunities of the Specialized Agencies. At the same time they continue to act as government representatives, reporting and receiving instructions from the Governments which selected them—in the case of Directors, representing more than one State, reporting to each of the States concerned.

[1] The privileges and immunities of the individual members of the executive organs of the ILO, UNESCO and WHO are referred to in the respective annexes to the Convention on the Privileges and Immunities of the Specialized Agencies. Such privileges and immunities may only be waived by the executive organ, not by the State concerned, thus denoting the supremacy of the international function.

[2] Article v, Section 4, Articles of Agreement. The Executive Directors of the International Monetary Fund are in a similar position.

Claims have been put forward designed to establish the importance of the 'Community' as opposed to 'national' functions of the Committee of Permanent Representatives at the European Economic Community. It is doubtful if the more extreme assertions made are altogether convincing or, if they are, that they are not self-defeating: the task of such Representatives is not only to perform acts on behalf of the Community but to do so in accordance with government instructions in such a manner as to ensure that any decisions taken will have the effective support of the State concerned. Unlike the position of, say, workers' and employers' delegates to the ILO Governing Body, the representation of state interest is a prerequisite to this *dédoublement de fonctions.* See Houben, *Les Conseils des Ministres des Communautés Européennes* (1964), pp. 124–5, and, generally, Noel, 'The Committee of Permanent Representatives', *Journal of Common Market Studies,* v (1967), p. 217.

Permanent representation

A distinct issue from that of the representation of States by specially qualified delegates or in particular organs is the establishment of a permanent mission at the seat of the organization concerned, as a means of enabling the State to follow day-to-day proceedings. This form of representation is now an accepted medium of diplomatic activity at all major international organizations.[1] Normally staffed by the foreign ministry and headed by someone of ambassadorial rank,[2] the main functions of these permanent delegations are: to serve on organs which meet at the headquarters of the organization (thus, at Brussels, the permanent representatives of Member States serve on the Committee of Permanent Representatives of the European Economic Community and Euratom); to provide a means of liaison with other permanent missions; and to maintain contact with the secretariat and to utilize its services (for example, as regards the dissemination of information between member States). The permanent missions of Member States at the United Nations, which received express recognition from the General Assembly in resolution 257A(III), adopted on 3 December 1948, perform these tasks in the light of the individual circumstances, such as whether the State concerned is a member of a given organ,[3] and the prevailing political situation in which the country may find itself. A distinction may be drawn here between the newly-independent States and others. By comparison with countries which had long possessed an extensive foreign service, the States which have become independent since the United Nations was established have relied on their United Nations contacts in order to obtain orientation, not so much regarding major lines of policy as on the innumerable items which go to make up the daily business of States. Discovering the views of kindred delegations, establishing at meetings of the regional caucus

[1] Such representation is to be found at the permanent offices of the following: the United Nations (New York and Geneva), the specialized Agencies, the Council of Europe, the European Communities, the Council of Mutual Economic Assistance (COMECON), the Arab League, the Organization of African Unity, the Organization of American States and the North Atlantic Treaty Organization.

[2] The Head of the United Kingdom Mission to the United Nations has ministerial rank and that of the United States Mission cabinet rank. Permanent missions of member States at international organizations, unlike bilateral diplomatic missions, enjoy the same status and are not graded according to the rank of their respective heads.

[3] Thus each member of the Security Council is required to be 'represented at all times at the seat of the Organization' (Article 28 of the Charter), so as to enable the Council to meet at short notice.

the common attitude to a particular issue which is about to come up—matters of this kind have been regularly discussed and elaborated at the site of United Nations Headquarters and of the offices of other international organizations before reaching the conference floor. Thus, far from it being the case that the national capital was determining policy in excessive detail, position papers have often been arrived at after being worked out in New York and then cleared at home.[1] Although the permanent missions of the other major groupings have performed similar functions, their role in the formation of policy has not usually been quite so direct. Their task, varying with the size and significance of the country, has been to ensure where possible the passage of resolutions in the form desired by the State or group concerned (this we may take to be the common object of all missions), and to report back on the attitudes of given countries on particular items, so that the ministry for foreign affairs may decide, for example, whether to alert its ambassadors in the field in an effort to get a change affected in the various national capitals, which in turn may cause a shift in vote at the United Nations.[2]

Other forms of representation: position of non-member States

Several other forms of representation should be noted in order to complete the picture. There are, for example, a number of organizations, or subordinate bodies of major organizations, to which States may detach liaison officers, usually members of the staff of the local embassy. This is the case at several of the United Nations regional economic commissions and it is the practice which is followed informally by certain East European countries as regards the European communities centred in Brussels. In such instances unless the person concerned is officially invited to attend a meeting of the organization in question his legal status is dependent on his position as a member of the embassy staff. A related form of representation, with more distinct characteristics, is that of an abserver, sent officially by a State to attend meetings and to follow the proceedings of an international organization. A distinction should be drawn between member and non-member States in that whereas the former may normally

[1] This generalization applies in inverse proportion to the size and importance of the country: the smaller the country the more likely this procedure is to be followed and, conversely, the more important the country the more likely that policy and instructions will be determined by the home authorities.

[2] For the inner workings of United Nations diplomacy see, in particular, Hoppenot, 'La diplomatie à l'intérieur des Nations Unies', *Les Nations Unies Chantier de l'avenir*, tome II (1961), p. 165, and Hadwen and Kaufmann, *How United Nations Decisions Are Made* (2 ed., 1962).

attend all meetings as of right, the position of non-member States is often more uncertain. In the case of an *ad hoc* meeting the convening organization, or possibly the conference itself, will usually determine whether observers of non-member States may attend. If, on the other hand, the non-member State wishes to follow the daily work of the organization, it may seek to establish a mission charged with observation functions on a permanent basis. The position of such missions varies from organization to organization, according to whether or not they or their staff are accredited to the organization and thus accorded an official status. A striking difference exists in this respect between the practice of the United Nations (for which non-member States represent very much the exception)[1] and that followed by the European Communities for whom, as bodies with a limited membership, non-member States form, so to speak, the norm. Before considering this issue further, however, it is necessary to examine more generally the question of the appointment and accreditation of missions and representatives.

APPOINTMENT AND ACCREDITATION

Unlike the position in the case of inter-state relations, a member State does not need to obtain the prior consent of the organization before entering into diplomatic relations with it (if the *petitio principi* as to whether such relations can be described as 'diplomatic' be permitted), nor does it require the *agrément* of the organization to the person it chooses to send. By virtue of its membership the State is entitled to claim representation within the limits envisaged under the terms of the constituent instrument, without it being a condition that, for example, the majority of other member countries recognize the State or Government in question for the purposes of bilateral diplomatic relations.[2] There is no difference in this respect between the dispatch of an *ad hoc* representative to a meeting of a given organ

[1] In 1967 there were six permanent observer missions at United Nations Headquarters: Federal Republic of Germany, Holy See, Republic of Korea, Monaco, Switzerland and Republic of Viet-Nam.

[2] See the Memorandum 'Legal Aspects of the Problem of Representation in the United Nations', A/1466 of 8 March 1950, and, generally, Liang, 'Recognition by the United Nations of the Representation of a Member State: Criteria and Procedure', *American Journal of International Law*, 45 (1951), p. 689. The formulation in the text is qualified by the fact that, since decisions as to representation are in most cases taken collectively (e.g. by majority vote), if most members do not recognize the State or Government concerned it is not likely that that State or Government will be permitted to remain represented indefinitely.

and the establishment of a permanent mission, where the analogy with a diplomatic mission applies more strongly.

Although formal consent is not a prerequisite, it still remains necessary to have some means which will enable other member States, and the organization itself, to ensure that the persons concerned are in fact empowered to act on behalf of the State which sent them. The procedure used is, in the case of *ad hoc* representatives, an adaptation of that used at international conferences, and, in the case of permanent missions, an adaptation of that observed with respect to embassy staff. Except as regards heads of State or Government and ministers of foreign affairs who, in accordance with established practice, require by definition no special proof of their title to represent their country, a delegate to a meeting of an international organization must normally present an instrument of credentials, signed by one of the three persons mentioned, stating that he is empowered to represent his country for the purpose in question. The formal authenticity of the credentials is considered by a small credentials committee or by the secretariat; a report is then submitted to the main body which makes the final ruling on a collective basis—a process which may well spill over to consideration of the authenticity of the Government concerned. In the case of the United Nations, if a State wishes its permanent representative to serve also as its representative on a given organ, such as the General Assembly or the Security Council, specific accreditation is required to that effect.[1]

As regards permanent representatives more generally, the issue arises of deciding to whom the head of a permanent mission should be accredited. When this matter was discussed by the Sixth Committee of the United Nations at the third session of the General Assembly in 1948 there was reluctance to name the Secretary-General for this purpose. It was felt that such action would elevate his role so as to make it too like that of a head of State, whilst also raising the question whether, and in what circumstances, he might decline to accept such accreditation. It was eventually concluded that, though the credentials should be transmitted to the Secretary-General, permanent representatives should simply be accredited to the Organization itself.[2] Despite the absence of a formal power of giving or withholding *agrément* with respect to individual appointments,

---

[1] Resolution 257A(III) of 3 December 1948.
[2] Thus, as noted, if permanent representatives are also to serve on special organs of the United Nations this must be specifically stated in the credentials issued.

the Secretary-General nevertheless fills some residual functions, including the receipt of credentials from incoming permanent representatives at a short ceremony arranged by the protocol section of the United Nations Secretariat. No corresponding procedure takes place in the case of the permanent observers appointed by non-member States, who are not formally accredited to the Organization. Except where a special invitation has been given by a United Nations organ—and no such invitation has yet been extended as regards the establishment of a permanent observer mission by a State—their status remains dependent on the attitude of the host State. The Secretary-General has several times asked the General Assembly to examine this question further, in order that he may be given a clear directive as to the Organization's policy with regard to the representation of non-member States, but so far no action has been taken.[1]

In the case of the United Nations non-member States represent the exception; for institutions with a limited membership, such as the European Communities, the position is reversed. Furthermore the extent and, indeed, the ambition of the conception of these Communities renders the question of their external relations of considerable political significance. The problems raised have touched on those jurisprudential issues concerning international legal personality and incipient federalism which European lawyers have debated so vigorously over the past ten years, in the course of the most important legal debate since Savigny and Thibault discussed the legal principles to govern the emerging German *Bund*. Taking the matter only from the standpoint of the right or capacity of the European Communities to receive representatives,[2] it is first necessary to distinguish the position of Member States. In the case of the appointment of representatives, whether to the various ministerial Councils or as permanent representatives, no authority or *agrément* is sought; the Member State simply nominates the person whom it has selected and brings the nomination to the knowledge of the

[1] *Introduction to the Annual Report of the Secretary-General on the Work of the Organization, 16 June 1963–15 June 1964* (A/5801/Add.1), p. 11, repeated in the *Introduction* issued in 1965 (A/6001/Add.1), p. 11, 1966 (A/6301/Add.1), p. 14, and 1967 (A/6701/Add.1), pp. 20–1.

[2] It may be noted that in a resolution adopted on 19 November 1960 the European Parliament expressed its opinion that 'les Communautés européennes jouissent de par leur personalité juridique internationale le droit de légation actif et passif'. *Assemblée Parlementaire Européenne, Débats, Avril 1961, No. 34, Session de Novembre 1960*, and idem., *Documents de Séance*, No. 87, 1959, and No. 88, 1960–1.

President of the Commission[1] and of the Council of the Community in question. Although the permanent representatives of Member States pay courtesy visits to the President of the Commission and to the acting President of the Council, they do not present credentials. In addition to the representatives of Member States, however, there is the question of the representation of the two categories of associate States. When Greece became an associate State, it requested that its representative be called a 'permanent delegate', to distinguish his status from that of the envoy of non-member States, a practice followed by Turkey when it too became an associate State. In the case of these full associate States, no agreement is required either as to the establishment of representation or as regards the individual delegate. The position is distinct therefore from that of the African States associated with the Community under the Convention of Yaoundé.[2] On gaining independence the latter States became autonomously associated members and as such invited to accredit a permanent mission. The missions concerned, which are given the special name of 'représentations', are subject to an accreditation procedure which is intermediate between that applied in the case of missions maintained by third States and that accorded with respect to the permanent representatives of Member States. A unilateral statement of the intention to enter into diplomatic relations is sent to the Community, followed by a letter, addressed to the Presidents of the Commission and the Council, nominating the person selected as representative. The Commission and the Council officially 'take note' of the designation within a specified period of thirty days. After the State has been informed of this fact by the Commission, its representative may begin his functions, following an official visit to the Presidents of the Commission and of the Council.

Non-member States, in the full sense of the term, form the last and largest category of countries maintaining permanent diplomatic representation at the European Communities. In their case it is

[1] In the case of the European Economic Community and Euratom. In the case of the European Coal and Steel Community the High Authority takes the place of the Commission. Attention is concentrated on the practice of the European Economic Community as being the most extensive and the most likely to be followed when the institutions of the three Communities are fused in accordance with the Treaty of 8 April 1965.

See, generally, Salmon, *Les représentations permanentes auprès de la C.E.E. et de l'EURATOM*, Centre européen de la Dotation Carnegie (1965).

[2] Signed on 20 July 1963. The Convention came into effect on 1 June 1964. The position of non-permanent representatives of associate States is not considered here.

necessary that a State which wishes to establish a permanent mission should first submit an application to the Director-General of the External Relations Section of the Secretariat of the Commission.[1] The request is examined and then submitted, with the Commission's recommendation, to the Council of Ministers; the Commission's application is deemed accepted if, within thirty days, the question is not put on the agenda of the next ministerial meeting. A similar procedure is followed with respect to the individuals proposed as heads of mission. Thus both the decision to establish relations and the *agrément* given to heads of missions are subject to the same requirements of consent as are observed between States. In the event of a favourable response, the incoming head of mission presents his credentials, in two original versions, on the same day and without ceremony, to the President of the Council and to the President of the Commission.[2]

THE GRANT OF PRIVILEGES AND IMMUNITIES

Whereas the legal status of representatives *vis-à-vis* the organization can be treated as a matter of internal regulation, to be collectively determined, the enjoyment of privileges and immunities requires the co-ordination of all three parties involved, namely the organization, the host State and the individual State concerned. Moreover, unlike traditional diplomatic law which has been based on custom, the legal provisions relating to the privileges and immunities to be accorded to state representatives at international organizations are primarily conventional. The most fundamental of the agreements concerned is normally the constitution of the organization itself. Article 105 of the United Nations Charter, for example, after stating that the Organization shall enjoy in the territory of its Members 'such privileges and immunities as are necessary for the fulfilment of its purposes', declares that the representatives of Member States 'shall similarly enjoy such privileges and immunities as are necessary

[1] In the case of the European Economic Community. Parallel arrangements exist with respect to the other two Communities. Some forty-eight States, in addition to Member and various Associate States, maintained permanent representation at the seat of the European Economic Community in 1966.

[2] Credentials were previously received solely by the President of the Commission at an impressive ceremony modelled on that observed by States. The change to the arrangement described in the text was agreed upon at the meeting of the Six Member States held in Luxembourg during January 1966; the modalities of the new arrangement were settled by an exchange of letters, dated 3 and 9 November 1966, between the President of the Council and the President of the Commission.

for the independent exercise of their functions in connexion with the Organization'. Similar articles are to be found in the constituent instrument of most other international organizations, so that accession to membership involves acceptance of the obligations derived from these clauses, as well as entitlement to their advantages. Supplementary agreements have also been drawn up, in order to give more precise guidance as to the contents of these statements of principle. Thus the Convention on the Privileges and Immunities of the United Nations, usually referred to as the 'General Convention', which was adopted on 13 February 1946, contains a chapter listing the privileges and immunities to be accorded to the representatives of Member States. A similar regime is laid down in the Specialized Agencies Convention and in the relevant agreements adopted by the majority of regional institutions. In addition to treaties of this character, which are intended to be applied generally by all States members of the particular organizations, it has been customary to enter into a special agreement with the State on whose territory the organization has its permanent offices. These host agreements as they are called[1] regulate in detail the position of the organization and of representatives to it in the country in question; not infrequently they are more generous in according privileges and immunities than the general agreement. Each of the instruments mentioned may be supplemented by the normal provisions of diplomatic law, either where, for example, the main agreement fails to provide for a familiar and necessary feature of the status of envoys, or more commonly, where the customary rule (now replaced by the Vienna Convention) are incorporated by reference as the standard of privileges and immunities to be afforded—a reference which may be either general in character[2] or relate solely to a particular privilege which is to be conferred.[3]

The fact that, in virtually all the instruments dealing with the privileges and immunities of international organizations provision is made for the granting to state representatives of a special status, akin if not identical with that accorded to diplomatic envoys, prompt the question whether an obligation to this effect now exists under

---

[1] Or 'headquarters agreement' in some cases, for example, the Agreement between the United Nations and United States of 26 June 1947.
[2] The approach followed in the various Protocols on privileges and immunities adopted by the European Communities; see, for example, Articles 11 and 17 of the Protocol of 8 April 1965.
[3] The method used in Article iv, Section 11(f) and (g), of the United Nations General Convention.

customary international law. The short answer is that probably such an obligation does exist, at least as regards the major organizations of universal vocation; in the case of organizations with more limited membership (and, usually, with more limited functions) it might be more difficult to establish that non-member States are under a positive duty to accord privileges and immunities, unless the third State involved was itself represented at the organization in question or at least friendly towards it.[1] The issue is denied great practical significance by the fact that any customary obligation which might be shown to exist probably does not extend beyond the requirement that only the most basic immunities, not amounting to full diplomatic advantages, are to be provided. Until a case arises squarely for decision therefore we can proceed on the assumption that the enjoyment of privileges and immunities depends on the terms of the relevant agreements, as interpreted in the practice chiefly of member States.

As regards the extent of the privileges and immunities which are accorded, a distinction should be drawn between permanent representatives and others. Taking first the position of *ad hoc* representatives, as a generalization, true of most but not all institutions, persons sent to attend meetings held at the offices of an organization receive privileges and immunities at a level below that accorded to diplomatic envoys exchanged between States. The exact difference will depend on a comparison between the relevant international agreement and the terms of the Vienna Convention (at least where the host State is a party to that instrument). In the case of the United Nations General Convention, which may be taken as the most influential summary of the position, the representatives of members are granted the following privileges 'while exercising their functions and during their journey to and from the place of meeting': (*a*) immunity from personal arrest or detention and, in respect of words spoken or acts done as representatives, immunity from legal process; (*b*)

---

[1] Thus, to take the question of the entry and transit of representatives—an essential privilege or facility—each Member State of the European Economic Community is obliged not to obstruct the passage of the representatives of fellow Members and, on *a priori* grounds, of the representatives of third States accredited to the Community. Is the United Kingdom also obliged under customary law to accord the same privilege: (*a*) to representatives of Member States of the Community; and (*b*) to the representatives of a third State also accredited to the Community; or (*c*) is the matter regulated exclusively by Article 40 of the Vienna Convention? That Article, in its terms, refers only to persons serving on bilateral diplomatic missions. And what is the position of a country, such as the USSR, which is not officially represented at the Community?

inviolability of papers and documents; (c) the right to use codes, diplomatic courier and diplomatic pouch; (d) exemption from immigration restrictions, alien registration and national service obligations; (e) the same facilities in respect of currency or exchange restrictions as the representatives of foreign Governments; (f) the same privileges and immunities as regards personal baggage as diplomatic envoys; and (g) 'such other privileges . . . not inconsistent with the foregoing as diplomatic envoys enjoy', subject to specified exceptions with respect to the payment of customs and excise duties and sales taxes.[1] The usual description of these privileges as 'functional' in character, by comparison with the 'diplomatic' status accorded to bilateral envoys is something of a misnomer in so far as the basis of the privileges and immunities accorded to ordinary diplomats is also primarily that of their function. It does, however, serve to emphasize the purpose for which the privileges are granted, namely in order to safeguard the independent exercise of the functions of representatives in connexion with the organization,[2] and provide a criterion against which to measure the need for privileges and immunities; consistent with this, the sending State is placed under an explicit obligation to waive the immunities enjoyed by its representatives where it can do so without prejudice to the purpose for which the immunity is granted. The 'functional' approach also underlines the interest of the organization in ensuring that representatives to it (both member and non-member States as the case may be) are not hindered in the performance of their tasks.

In the case of permanent representatives, on the other hand, assimilation, so far as local law is concerned, to diplomatic status forms the general rule. Since this involves not merely immunity in respect of acts performed in an official capacity but the grant of complete immunity from jurisdiction, the position of the host State is correspondingly more exposed. Unlike the position with respect to diplomats received in the course of bilateral relations, the host State has no say (except, of course, as one of the member States of the organization)[3] as to whether the State shall maintain its representation, nor over the particular individual selected; nor, furthermore,

---

[1] Article IV, Section 11. None of the privileges and immunities listed are applicable as between the representative and the State of which he is a national or of which he is, or has been, a representative.

[2] So stated in Article IV, Section 14, of the General Convention. The adoption of this provision constituted the first major inroad in the classical 'representational' theory.   [3] And not always that, as in the case of Switzerland as regards representatives at the United Nations Office at Geneva.

does the host State have the right which it possesses in the case of diplomats accredited to itself, of declaring a particular representative no longer *persona grata*. Host States have accordingly sought to reserve to themselves certain residual powers as to whether or not, and the conditions under which, they are prepared to grant full diplomatic privileges and immunities. At the same time no host State has claimed a unilateral right to control the appointments made by other member (or even non-member) States—although the distinction may well grow fine on occasions. The issue which presents itself therefore is that of allocating the degrees of interest of the sending State and of the organization on the one hand (which will be primarily concerned to maintain their freedom from outside interference) and of the host State on the other (which will be concerned in the last resort with safeguarding its national security). In practice, the question is posed in the following form: What acts must be performed by the individual State, the organization, and the host State respectively, before full diplomatic privileges and immunities are granted—is such a grant to be made automatically by the host State upon notification (in which case, from whom is the notification to come), or does the host State have an independent voice in the matter? Three positions, each of which shows some variation, may be noted, according to the terms of the relevant texts in force at United Nations Headquarters in New York, at the United Nations Office at Geneva, and at the European organizations in Brussels and Luxembourg. Each of these will be examined in turn.

United Nations Headquarters

At United Nations Headquarters in New York the only relevant agreement, apart from the Charter itself, is the Headquarters Agreement, concluded between the Organization and the United States in 1947. That Agreement deals chiefly with the permanent representatives (here referred to as 'resident representatives') of Member States.[1] Section 15 of the Agreement provides that

[1] *Ad hoc* representatives to meetings held at United Nations Headquarters are entitled to the benefits derived from Article 105, paragraph 2, of the Charter, but not to those specified in the General Convention, to which the United States is not a party. A statute, the International Organizations Immunities Act (59 Stat. 669 (1945), 22 U.S.C. Sec. 288 (1952)), was enacted in 1945 before the adoption of the General Convention with the object of fulfilling the United States' obligations under Article 105. The privileges and immunities granted to foreign representatives under that Act principally include 'immunity from suit and legal process relating to acts performed by them in their official capacity and falling within their functions' (Section 7(*b*)), immunity from taxation and immunity from im-

(*i*) Every person designated by a Member as the principal resident representative to the United Nations of such Member or as a resident representative with the rank of ambassador or minister plenipotentiary,

(*ii*) Such other resident members of their staffs as may be agreed upon between the Secretary-General, the Government of the United States and the Government of the Member concerned,

shall be entitled to 'the same privileges and immunities, subject to corresponding conditions and obligations, as (the United States) accords to diplomatic envoys accredited to it'. Thus, whereas the only requirement for the grant of privileges and immunities to the head of the mission is that he be 'designated' by the Member State, a tripartite agreement is envisaged with respect to subordinate members of the staff. In resolution 169B(II) of 31 October 1947, the General Assembly recommended to the Secretary-General and to the United States authorities that, in considering 'what *classes of persons* on the staff of delegations might be included in the lists to be drawn up by agreement between the Secretary-General, the Government of the United States of America and the Government of the Member concerned' (italics added), Section 16 of the General Convention, which specifies the major categories of diplomatic staff,[1] should be used as a guide. In accordance with this recommendation the Secretary-General wrote to all Member States in December 1947, informing them that the Headquarters Agreements had come into effect and requesting them to forward the lists of the persons covered by Section 15(1) and (2); these lists were then transmitted by the Secretary-General to the United States authorities. The Secretary-General subsequently reported to the General Assembly that the list of persons falling upon Section 15(2) had been 'established . . . by tripartite agreement' between the three parties concerned and that 'the criterion recommended by the General Assembly concerning the classes of persons on the personnel of the delegations to be included' had been observed.[2] In following years

---

migration and certain other entry restrictions. The benefits of the Act are dependent on the condition that the person concerned 'shall have been duly notified to and accepted by the Secretary of State as a representative' (Section 8(*a*)). The Headquarters Agreement, which came into force in 1947, supersedes the 1945 enactment as regards the position of permanent representatives generally and, as regards *ad hoc* representatives, with respect to entry and transit.

[1] Section 16 provides that 'the expression "representatives" shall be deemed to include all delegates, deputy delegates, advisers, technical experts and secretaries of delegations'.

[2] *Report of the Secretary-General on the Privileges and Immunities of the United Nations*, A/626, 7 September 1948.

the practice has been for the Secretary-General to forward to the United States the name and relevant particulars of persons falling within those classes as changes have occurred in mission staff (or as new States have entered the Organization), so that the relevant privileges and immunities may be granted.

The extent and nature of the tripartite agreement became in issue in the case of *United States Ex. Rel. Roberto Santiesteban Casanova v. Fitzpatrick*[1] which, since it raised a point of principle, deserves attention. Mr. Santiesteban entered the United States on 3 October 1962, with a Cuban diplomatic passport bearing a United States visa, in order to take up his duties as an attaché at the Cuban Permanent Mission to the United Nations. Having been notified of his arrival, the United Nations forwarded his name to the State Department on 15 October. Approximately a month later he was arrested while attending a meeting of Cuban nationals and charged with conspiring to commit espionage. Two other Cuban attachés were named as co-conspirators, together with certain persons unnamed. Since the two attachés had been accepted earlier by the United States, the host authorities merely requested that they be recalled by the Government of the sending State. Mr. Santiesteban, however, was held on indictment on the ground that consent to the grant of diplomatic privileges and immunities had not yet been accorded by the United States. He petitioned for a writ of habeas corpus, claiming that his imprisonment was illegal under the terms of Article 105 of the Charter, customary international law and Section 15 of the Headquarters Agreement; he also sought the benefits of the exclusive jurisdiction of the Supreme Court over cases affecting diplomats. The Court dismissed the petition. It held that Article 105 of the Charter did not require that complete jurisdictional immunity be granted and that customary law was inapplicable since the immunity of United Nations representatives was governed solely by statute and agreement. Nor, since Mr. Santiesteban was not accredited to the United States, could his case fall under the original jurisdiction of the Supreme Court.[2] The Court

---

[1] U.S.Dist.Ct.S.D.N.Y. 16 January 1963. 214 F. Suppl. p. 425. While his case was pending appeal Mr. Santiesteban was repatriated, pursuant to a special agreement, in exchange for a United States national held by the Cuban Government. *New York Times*, 23 April 1963, p. 1, col. 6 and 25 April 1963, p. 1, col. 7. See also *United Nations Juridical Yearbook, 1963*, p. 200, footnote.

[2] For criticism of this aspect of the Court's reasoning see 'United States Jurisdiction over Representatives to the United Nations', *Columbia Law Review*, LXIII (1963), p. 1066, at pp. 1077, 1081.

flatly rejected the argument presented that the agreement envisaged under Section 15(2) referred to classes and not to individuals. In doing so the Court acknowledged that it was influenced by the statement of the State Department that agreement had been refused on at least five occasions in the past. It is not clear, however, whether these cases of refusal were instances in which the United States refused to grant diplomatic privileges and immunities to individuals falling within an accepted class or whether they turned on questions relating to classes (for example, whether or not a particular category of persons, such as chancellery staff, were to be included). The basic question, as to whether the agreement referred to in Section 15(2) refers to individuals or to classes thus remains an open one.

So far as the United Nations is concerned, acceptance of the argument of the Court would entail as a logical consequence that the Secretary-General also has a power of individual consent or refusal—a power which, as regards accreditation at least, the Sixth Committee was anxious in 1948 not to concede. In the particular case, the question may also be posed: if Mr. Santiesteban was not accepted for the purposes of Section 15 of the Headquarters Agreement, what privileges and immunities did he receive? Under the United States International Organizations Act, adopted in 1945, he would be entitled to functional immunities (not including immunity from arrest) but in that case also, beneficiaries must be 'duly notified to and accepted by' the Secretary of State. At the very least he must have been entitled to the benefits of Article 105, paragraph 2, granting representatives 'such privileges and immunities as are necessary for the independent exercise of their functions'. Paragraph 3 of Article 105 states that the General Assembly may make recommendations with a view to determining the details of the application of the preceding paragraphs of the Article. Whilst the General Convention, which was adopted in pursuance of this provision, specifies that the immunity from legal process of representatives is confined to acts done in their official capacity, the immunity from personal arrest or detention which is granted is not so qualified. Since the United States is not a party to the General Convention[1] no question arises of a conflict between that instrument on the one hand and the Headquarters Agreement and the International Organizations Act on the other, although there is, as the facts of the *Santiesteban* case show, a discrepancy. If the United States should accede to the General

---

[1] Although the General Convention and the Headquarters Agreement are stated in Section 26 of the latter to be complementary.

Convention this discordance would be removed—though it would still leave the question of the nature of the agreement envisaged in Section 15(2) unresolved.[1]

The position of representatives of non-member States at U.N. Headquarters is more straightforward. Whilst the Headquarters Agreement contains no express reference to them *eo nomine*, the United States authorities are obliged under Article IV to grant them the right of transit if they are invited to U.N. Headquarters on official business. In the absence of such invitation they are dependent on the 1945 International Organizations Immunities Act which declares that 'persons designated by foreign governments to serve as their representatives in or to international organizations'[2] may receive immunity from suit in respect of their official functions, and the other privileges specified, provided the individual concerned has been accepted by the Secretary of State. The phrase 'in or *to* international organizations' (italics added) has been interpreted to provide the representatives of non-member States with the benefits conferred by that statute; any privileges and immunities given in excess of the statutory minimum have been granted solely as a matter of courtesy.

United Nations Office at Geneva

The 1946 Agreement between the United Nations and Switzerland provides representatives of Member States 'on its principal and subsidiary organs and at conferences convened by the United Nations' with the same privileges and immunities as are accorded under the General Convention.[3] No mention is made in that Agreement, nor in any Swiss legislation, that these representatives are subject to the consent of the host authorities before they may enjoy the benefits which are accorded. In the case of permanent representatives and members of their staff, a Decision of the Swiss Federal Council of 31 March 1948 grants privileges and immunities analogous to those accorded to diplomatic personnel accredited to Berne. To receive the advantages of the Decision it is necessary that members of the staff should be able to perform their functions in Geneva on a

---

[1] The possibility of a case similar to the *Santiesteban* one recurring has been reduced by an administrative procedure introduced in 1964 whereby permanent missions may submit names of new staff in advance. *The Practice of the United Nations, the Specialized Agencies and the International Atomic Energy Agency, concerning their Status, Privileges and Immunities*, A/CN.4/L.118, paragraph 65.

[2] Section 7(*a*), International Organizations Immunities Act. See also *United Nations Juridical Yearbook, 1962*, p. 236, and *Pappas v. Francini, International Law Reports*, vol. 25, p. 380. [3] Agreements in similar terms have been concluded with the specialized agencies having their principal offices in Switzerland.

permanent basis. Before the *carte de légitimation*, which attests the grant of diplomatic privileges and immunities, is issued by the Federal Political Department, the certification of the Director-General of the Geneva Office is required that the particular individual is a member of a permanent mission accredited to that Office.[1] In order to be in a position to provide such certification the Director-General must be satisfied that the person is to reside permanently in Geneva during the period of his assignment and is to work continuously for the permanent mission. Thus a person who will be in Geneva only intermittently, for the purposes of attending certain conferences or meetings, will be excluded. Instances where the individual concerned is not a national of the country which he is appointed to represent are examined with especial care since, although the restrictions contained in Article 8 of the Vienna Convention are inapplicable for United Nations purposes, it is undesirable that persons should be granted diplomatic privileges and immunities in the host State when appointed to the mission solely in an honorary capacity.

In the case of *B v. M.* the Swiss Federal Tribunal declined to acknowledge the jurisdictional immunity which was claimed by an Iranian national in a private suit, despite the submission of a statement by the Permanent Representative of Iran declaring that the defendant had been appointed a member of his staff.[2] Noting that the competent federal authorities had not been notified, nor appropriate recognition shown by those authorities to the appointment, that Court held that, in the circumstances, there was no valid basis for the immunity which was claimed.

In the case of non-member States, as in New York, there is no international agreement which expressly regulates the grant of privileges and immunities. In the absence of a special invitation by a United Nations body, the position of the representatives of such States is therefore dependent on the attitude of the Host State. Permanent observers of non-member States stationed at the United Nations Office at Geneva[3] are granted the same *de facto* status as the observers of Member States, who in turn are treated in much the same way as the representatives of Member States.

---

[1] *United Nations Juridical Yearbook, 1965*, p. 222. The wording of the 1948 Decision, which refers to notification through the diplomatic mission in Berne, has been largely superseded by the procedure referred to in the text.

[2] *International Law Reports*, vol. 27, p. 254.

[3] Except in the case of the Permanent Observer maintained since 1966 at the Geneva Office by the Swiss Federal Political Department.

European Communities at Brussels and Luxembourg

At the European Communities in Brussels and Luxembourg the respective Host States are bound by international agreements providing for the grant of 'the customary privileges, immunities and facilities' to the representatives of Member States and their staff[1] and of 'customary diplomatic immunities' to the missions of third States accredited to the Communities.[2] In the case of Member and Associate States, privileges and immunities are granted by Belgium and Luxembourg upon notice; the relevant provisions of the Vienna Convention are applied in the usual way. The representatives of third States receive privileges and immunities following notification to the respective Foreign Ministries of Belgium and Luxembourg, sent by the Commissions in the case of the European Economic Community and of Euratom and by the High Authority in the case of the Coal and Steel Community, after the Communities have agreed to accept the representative of the State in question. The privileges and immunities granted are analogous to those received by the diplomatic mission accredited to Belgium and Luxembourg by the third State; if the third State does not maintain diplomatic relations with these countries its mission will, it is thought, be given the standard of treatment accorded by the other Member States to which it is accredited.[3] Thus, only at the European Communities are the

[1] The respective Protocols on the Privileges and Immunities of the European Economic Community, Euratom and of the European Coal and Steel Community, contain identical provisions (Article 10) on this point; the Protocol of the Privileges and Immunities of the European Communities, signed on 8 April 1965, repeats the provision in Article 11.

[2] In the case of the European Economic Commission and Euratom this is so provided in Article 17 of the respective Protocols on Privileges and Immunities. No corresponding provision was included in the first Protocol concluded, relating to Euratom. By a Law adopted on 7 August 1956, Luxembourg agreed to grant the same privileges and immunities as were accorded to the diplomatic missions of the same State accredited to Luxembourg; see United Nations Legislative Series, *Legislative Texts and Treaty Provisions concerning the Legal Status, Privileges and Immunities of International Organizations* (1961), vol. II, pp. 37, 405. The Protocol on the Privileges and Immunities of the European Communities of 8 April 1965, replaces these arrangements with a single uniform provision in Article 17.

In the case of Belgium it may be noted that an instruction of the Ministry of Finance (1962, titre III, no. 207) declares that the advantages granted to missions established within the Belgian-Luxembourg Economic Union and which are accredited to international organizations there, 's'établissent sous les mêmes conditions et dans les mêmes limites que celles qui régissent les immunités diplomatiques proprement dites'.

[3] At least in the case of the European Economic Community, per Salmon, op. cit., p. 16.

representatives of non-member States fully protected by an international agreement binding on the host State—and only at these
organizations are the representatives of third States accredited as
such to an international body.

SPECIAL PROBLEMS WITH RESPECT TO PRIVILEGES
AND IMMUNITIES

Reciprocity

The operation of the principle of reciprocity in bilateral diplomatic
relations is recognized in the Vienna Convention;[1] what application,
if any, should it have with respect to representatives at international
organizations? As was suggested in a report to the European Parlia-
mentary Assembly, only the organization, as the receiving entity,
can properly assert or enforce reciprocity by balancing the position
of the representatives which it itself sends against that of the representatives which it receives.[2] The dispatch of envoys by international
organizations is a rare occurrence, however, and, since the grant of
privileges and immunities by representatives accredited to international organizations remains cast in terms of the law of the host
State, even in that case, reciprocity could not be applied directly.
The position of the host State remains crucial.

There are two main considerations to be borne in mind. Firstly,
as a matter of principle, the host country is under an obligation not
to differentiate in the treatment it accords to the representatives of
the various individual States represented at the organization. As
was said with reference to the United Nations by the Legal Adviser
of the United States Department of State: 'the purpose of the
Charter in respect of Article 105 is to provide for the granting un-
conditionally by Member States of certain privileges and immunities
to the United Nations so that it may function effectively as a world

[1] Article 47, paragraph 2. See p. 83 above.
[2] *Assemblée Parlementaire Européenne. Rapport fait au nom de la Commission
des affaires politiques et des questions institutionnelles sur les problèmes que posent
les relations des Communautés européennes avec l'extérieur, en particulier le droit
de légation et de pavillon, par M. van der Goes van Naters, rapporteur.* Doc. No. 87,
1959, pp. 3–4. In an exchange of notes with the High Authority of the European
Coal and Steel Community Luxembourg agreed that the application of privileges
to the missions of non-member States accredited to the High Authority should be
dependent on the provision of reciprocal treatment to the missions sent by the
High Authority. United Nations Legislative Series, *Legislative Texts and Treaty
Provisions concerning the Legal Status, Privileges and Immunities of International
Organizations* (1961), vol. II, p. 405. Note also the terms of the 1962 instruction
of the Belgian Ministry of Finance, quoted in note 2, p. 116 above.

organization untrammelled in its operation by national requirements of reciprocity or national measures of retaliation among States'.[1] Whilst this is particularly clear in the case of universal organizations, it is evident that no inter-governmental institution of however limited a size could long operate unless the representatives of all members were equally unfettered in the performance of their functions. Secondly, under the terms of the host agreement or other instrument the host country may agree to grant privileges and immunities to representatives (usually only to permanent representatives) analogous to those which it grants to the envoys accredited to itself, and subject to the same conditions. This is the position in New York, Geneva, Paris, Rome, Vienna and Brussels for example, with respect to the permanent representatives accredited to the organizations which have their permanent offices in those cities. Thus although, as in bilateral relations, reciprocity in the curtailment of privileges and immunity cannot be applied with regard to essential matters, such as the duty to provide protection and jurisdictional immunity in respect of acts performed in an official capacity, the host State may on occasions decline to extend full diplomatic privileges to the representatives of given States on the ground that the representatives of those States accredited to the national capital are subject to similar restrictions. The circumstances in which this interpretation can be applied depend, however, on the bilateral relations between the host country and the individual countries concerned. For example, where State A imposes restrictions on the freedom of movement of diplomats from State B accredited to it, State B may retaliate in kind by setting corresponding limits on the freedom of movement of A's diplomats which it itself receives. If State B is also the host State of an organization where A has stationed representatives, may it impose similar restrictions on them? Basing itself on the wording of the Headquarters Agreement, which provides that resident representatives to the United Nations shall be 'entitled in the territory of the United States to the same privileges and immunities, subject to corresponding conditions and obligations, as it accords to diplomatic envoys accredited to it', the United States has in fact imposed restrictions on the movements of representatives of East European countries accredited to the United Nations, as well as those accredited to Washington, in reply to the imposition of restrictions on the movements of United States diplo-

---

[1] *Structure of the United Nations and the Relations of the United States to the United Nations. Hearings before the Committee on Foreign Affairs. House of Representatives, Eightieth Congress, Second Session*, p. 508.

mats stationed in those countries.[1] Whatever the strength of the argument which may be placed on terms of the particular head-quarters agreement,[2] there can be no doubt that, from the standpoint of the organization, such actions are to be regretted. It is not the purpose of establishing an organization in a particular State to enable that country, by the mere fact that it is the host State, to exercise an additional means of pressure on other States for purposes which relate to its bilateral relations with them—at the expense of good relations within the membership of the organization of which it is the host. The organization would accordingly be justified in protesting to the host State in the event that it considered the discrimination in treatment being accorded to the representatives of different Member States was affecting its ability to achieve its objectives.

Non-recognition by the host State of a State or Government represented at an international organization

The fact that the host State does not, in its bilateral relations, recognize a State or Government represented, or wishing to be represented, at an international organization, is in principle irrelevant to the right of the latter State to maintain such representation. In a classic statement the Swiss Federal Council informed the League of Nations that it had

... always held as a universal principle that the existing relations between the Government of the country in which the League of Nations is established, or of any country in which the League may from time to time arrange meetings, and the Government of any country, whether a Member of the League of Nations or not, should in no way influence the possibility of untrammelled negotiations between the organs of the League of Nations and the representatives of the last-named State; nor should the co-operation between the League of Nations and any State directly influence the relations between that State and the country in which the League of Nations is established, or in which a conference may be held under the auspices of the League.[3]

---

[1] *Department of State Bulletin*, 49 (1963), p. 855 and p. 860. Contrastingly, when the Swiss Political Department considered the question of the grant of customs facilities to permanent missions, it declared that it would be difficult to make the grant conditional upon reciprocity, as in the case of foreign missions at Berne, since permanent missions 'are not accredited to the Swiss Government but are delegations of States Members of the United Nations, who have equal rights and are not subject to discrimination amongst them by the Swiss Government'. United Nations, *Handbook on the Legal Status, Privileges and Immunities of the United Nations* (ST/LEG/2) (1952), pp. 221 and 249.

[2] In the case of the Headquarters Agreement with the United States, see the opinion of the Legal Adviser of the State Department referred to in note 1, p.118 above, at p. 511.   [3] League of Nations Official Journal, March 1926, p. 488.

The general position may be qualified, however, under the terms of the pertinent agreement between the organization and the host State, such as that between the United Nations and the United States which provides that, although no impediment shall be placed on transit to or from the headquarters district, irrespective of the relations existing between the Member State concerned and the United States,[1] the diplomatic privileges and immunities granted to the resident representatives of Governments unrecognized by the United States shall extend 'only within the headquarters district, at their residences and offices outside the district, in transit between the district and such residences and offices, and in transit on official business to or from foreign countries'.[2]

The status of representatives of States which are neither members of the organization nor recognized by the host country is especially precarious. In the case of United Nations such representatives can neither obtain diplomatic privileges and immunities nor, unless specially invited, even a right of transit to United Nations offices, unless the host State agrees to accord these facilities as a matter of courtesy. At the European Communities no formal distinction has been drawn according to whether or not the host State (or any other Member) has recognized a particular third State which wishes to be represented. When, however, the Republic of China, having previously been given consent to establish a mission, sought the *agrément* of the European Economic Community for the individual it proposed to send, this was opposed by one of the Member States which had, during the intervening period, withdrawn recognition of the Government concerned. On the other hand, the Belgian Government continued to accord full privileges and immunities to the Congolese Representative after diplomatic relations had been broken off between the two countries.[3] It would be a very sizeable sanction for members of the 'Six' if, besides ending bilateral relations, they could also interrupt those maintained at Brussels—the very fact that such a possibility (unlikely, but nevertheless a possibility) can be discussed illustrates once more the difference between the loose-knit, universal bodies, such as the United Nations, and those with limited membership and, in this case, quasi-federal characteristics.

A dispute which arose in 1966 over certain premises occupied by

---

[1] Section 12. See p. 122 below.

[2] Section 15, *in fine*. A similar provision is contained in Section 24(*b*) of the Agreement between Italy and the Food and Agriculture Organization.

[3] Salmon, op. cit., pp. 18–19.

the Mission of the Republic of China to UNESCO, title to which was said to vest in the Chinese State, illustrates a special point of difficulty as regards the recognition, or non-recognition, of a given Member State or Government by the host State.[1] In March 1966 the French authorities entered and took possession of the premises and forcibly removed the members of the staff. In reply to the protest made by the Director-General of UNESCO the French Government declared that the buildings in question belonged to the Chinese State, which the Embassy of the People's Republic of China was alone entitled to represent in France. The French Government had not taken 'legal cognizance' of a purported transfer of the premises from the former Embassy of the Republic of China to its UNESCO Mission; consequently, the Mission had no legal title to justify its occupation of the premises and did not therefore enjoy any immunity in respect of its possession of them. The Mission had been asked on a number of occasions to vacate the premises and had been offered alternative accommodation, which it had refused to accept. The recognition by France of the Government of the People's Republic of China brought into being 'an international obligation for the French Government, which could not thereafter tolerate the totally unwarranted occupation of buildings belonging to the Chinese State, against the will of that State, which is the legitimate owner'. The Director-General of UNESCO, in the course of an exchange of notes, pointed out that under Article 18 of the Headquarters Agreement between France and UNESCO, the head of a mission of a Member State enjoyed the status accorded to heads of foreign diplomatic missions; the premises occupied as the headquarters of a delegation or as the domicile of a head of mission were therefore inviolable. This point of view was in conformity with international practice, as codified in Article 22 of the Vienna Convention.[2] The latter provisions did not 'make the inviolability of the premises of a delegation's headquarters dependent on the recognition, by the Government of the State on whose territory the premises are situated, of a title of ownership'. The issue of inviolability, as provided under the Headquarters Agreement, was therefore distinguished from that of

[1] UNESCO Executive Board, 72nd Session. Docs. 72 EX/11, 13 April 1966, 72/EX/11 Add., 20 April 1966, and 72/EX/Decisions, Item 9.1. When the item was placed before the Executive Board several members declared that the question involved was one within the competence of the French Government and should not therefore be considered by the Board. The resolution adopted on 13 May 1966 (see p. 122 below) received twelve votes in favour, one against and nine abstentions. [2] See p. 43 above.

ownership; the conflict over the latter was said not to concern the Organization, but solely the Government of the Republic of China and the Government of France.

The difference of opinion between the Host State and UNESCO, as to whether the measures taken by the French authorities were or were not in conformity with the Headquarters Agreement, was referred to the UNESCO Executive Board for judgement. The Board adopted a resolution in which it noted with appreciation the attitude of the Director-General and expressed its confidence that he would safeguard the provisions of the Headquarters Agreement, but did not otherwise comment on the legal issues raised.

Right of entry, transit and sojourn

The right of representatives to cross the territory of the host and other States when in transit to the meeting place of the organization, and to reside in the locality, is an essential condition to the performance of their tasks. Member States, under general principles, are bound to allow the representatives of fellow members, or the representatives of non-member States, entities or individuals, to exercise this right when authorized to do so under the rules of the organization. In the case of representatives of Member States of the United Nations, this right is derived from Article 105 of the Charter and forms a corollary of the principle of sovereign equality to which all Members are entitled under Article 2, paragraph 1, of that instrument. The essential element in the right of access is that representatives of Governments and other persons invited on official business shall not be impeded in their transit to or from the United Nations offices in connexion with meetings or other activities in which they are entitled to participate. Although this does not mean that the representatives of Member States have a right of entry to every United Nations office at any time, it clearly means that such right of access to United Nations premises must be granted to representatives of Members at least when they are entitled to attend meetings held in such premises or are invited to such premises in connexion with the official business of the Organization. This also implies that representatives of Member States and other persons having official business with the Organizations should have the right to communicate freely with United Nations offices by mail, telephone or telegraph.[1]

Express provisions have been included in the major 'site' and conference agreements so as to ensure the unhindered exercise of this right. The Headquarters Agreement of the International Atomic Energy Agency, for example, provides that the Austrian Govern-

[1] 'Legal Opinion of the United Nations Secretariat', *United Nations Juridical Yearbook, 1963*, p. 167.

ment shall place 'no impediment in the way of transit to or from the headquarters seat and shall accord . . . any necessary protection in transit' to all persons having official business with the Organization (including the representatives of non-member States sent as observers to meetings convened by the Agency).[1] The right of access and transit thus has as its corollary the freedom from interference which transit or host States are required to accord to the representatives of Member States who are travelling to or from United Nations meetings. This aspect came to the fore in 1967 during a dispute in which the Ivory Coast detained the Foreign Minister and Permanent Representative to the United Nations of Guinea after their plane had been forced, owing to bad weather, to land in the Ivory Coast. The Guinea officials were returning from the Fifth emergency special session of the General Assembly. The Secretary-General offered his good offices to the two States and drew attention to the obligations imposed under Section 11 of the General Convention. Under that provision the representatives of Member States attending United Nations meetings or conferences enjoy, *inter alia*, immunity from arrest or detention 'during their journey to and from the place of meeting'. The persons concerned were eventually released. In view of the significance of the principle involved the question of 'reaffirmation of an important immunity' of representatives was placed on the agenda, at the request of the Secretary-General, and considered by the General Assembly at its Twenty-second session in 1967.[2]

Differences have also occurred, however, where a host State has denied access to United Nations premises on the ground that the relevant agreement is subject to a reservation designed to safeguard national security, or that the host State does not recognize the Government in question. While no problem has arisen at United Nations Headquarters with respect to the representatives of Member States, the relevant provisions[3] were discussed in connexion with the refusal by the United States in 1953 to grant entry visas to certain representatives of non-governmental organizations.[4] In support of its position the United States invoked Section 6 of the Law authorizing the President to bring the Headquarters Agreement into effect[5] as

[1] Article XI, Section 27.
[2] See the Secretary-General's report, S/8120, 14 August 1967, and *General Assembly Official Records, Twenty-second session, Annexes*, agenda item 98.
[3] Article IV, Headquarters Agreement.
[4] See *Repertory of Practice of United Nations Organs*, vol. V, pp. 343–5, and idem, *Supplement No. 1*, vol. II, p. 423, where detailed references may be found.
[5] Public Law 357, 80th Congress, 1st Session, 61 Stat. 756.

constituting a reservation to the Agreement; the Section provides that nothing in the Agreement shall be construed as diminishing in any way the right of the United States to safeguard its own security and to control the entrance of aliens into the United States, other than to the United Nations headquarters district and its immediate vicinity. Although the Secretary-General[1] drew attention to the provisions of this Section prior to the adoption of a resolution by the General Assembly authorizing the Secretary-General to bring the Agreement into operation, the United Nations had not accepted that the right of transit which that Agreement provides had been made subject to a reservation.[2] The Organization did not therefore concede that the United States had the authority which it claimed, namely to restrict transit to and from the headquarters district on grounds of national security. Negotiations were held with the United States authorities by the Secretary-General in order to see whether a satisfactory result could be achieved by agreement. After a report had been submitted to the Economic and Social Council, the organ whose meetings the representatives concerned had wished to attend, a resolution was adopted expressing the Council's trust that any remaining questions would be settled within the provisions of the Headquarters Agreement. Whilst it cannot be said that the dispute has been clearly resolved no recent cases of denial of access have occurred with respect to persons having official business with the Organization.

Although the cases which occurred at United Nations Headquarters did not concern the entry of the representatives of Member States, so as to raise the question to what extent reservations on grounds of national security are compatible with the obligations under constituent instruments that such representatives are to be accorded all necessary privileges and immunities, this issue has been posed in at least one other case. From 1949 on Egypt refused to grant the necessary visa to the representatives of Israel who wished to attend meetings at the Alexandria office of the World Health Organization, in reliance on a reservation in the host agreement that 'the

[1] *Report by the Secretary-General on the Agreement between the United Nations and the United States regarding the Headquarters of the United Nations*, A/371, 3 September 1947.
[2] See the legal opinion given by the United Nations Secretariat, E/2397, Economic and Social Council Official Records, 15th Session, Annexes, Agenda item 34, and also the account given by Gross in 'Immunities and Privileges of Delegations to the United Nations', *International Organization*, 16 (1962), p. 483, at pp. 493–9.

Egyptian Government may take, as regards nationals of countries whose relations with Egypt are not normal, all precautions necessary for the security of the country'.[1] The World Health Assembly invited Egypt to reconsider the matter, and in 1954 Egypt withdrew the reservation. In a further case which arose in 1960, Pakistan declined to issue a visa to the observer designated by Israel to the session of the Economic Commission for Asia and the Far East which was due to be held in Karachi. The Secretary-General therefore arranged for the venue of the meeting to be changed to one where access by all Member States was ensured.[2] Where, however, a collective decision is taken, in accordance with the rules of the organization, the effect of which is to deny the right of representation or attendance to a given State, no right of entry or transit can be claimed. The compatibility of any action so taken with the rules and guiding principles of the organization is a matter lying outside the scope of the present lectures.

Abuse of privileges and immunities

In the case of representatives to an international organization, unlike that of normal diplomatic envoys, the application of the *persona non grata* doctrine does not lie in the hands of the host State, to whom the representatives are not of course accredited. Thus, apart from instances of the withdrawal or change of representatives at the initiative of the member State concerned or as a result of action taken by the organization (for example, to expel a particular State) when the usual rules apply as to the expiry of privileges and immunity after a reasonable period, the host State cannot itself usually take steps to require the representative of a given State to leave or terminate unilaterally the privileges he receives. Conceivably, if the representative is separately accredited to the host State, that State might declare him *persona non grata* if it disliked this double accreditation.

Nevertheless, since the host State has no direct control over the appointment of representatives, it has been customary to make provision in the relevant agreements for the possibility of abuse. The representatives to an international organization are not entitled, any more than those accredited to a State, to disregard local law or to interfere in the internal affairs of the host State. Although the

[1] Official Records of WHO, No. 35, Annex 7, p. 282. See on this and several other cases, Goy, 'Le droit d'accès au siège des organisations internationales', *Revue générale de droit international public*, LXVI (1962), p. 357.

[2] United Nations Note to Correspondents, No. 2099, 19 January 1960, and Goy, idem.

United Nations General Convention contains no article directly on the point, a Member State 'not only has the right, but is under a duty' to waive the immunity of its representative where the course of justice would otherwise be impeded and the waiver would not prejudice the purpose for which the immunity is accorded.[1] The Specialized Agencies Convention deals with the matter more specifically. If a State party to the Convention considers that there has been an abuse of a privilege or immunity conferred, consultations are to be held between that State and the specialized agency concerned; if a mutually satisfactory result is not achieved, the question may be referred to the International Court of Justice.[2] If the Court finds that an abuse has occurred the State member may withhold from the specialized agency the benefits of the privilege abused. Whilst this provision is primarily (though not exclusively) directed against the possibility of abuse by the specialized agency itself, Section 25 of the Convention provides that the representatives of members shall not be required by the territorial authorities to leave the country in which they are performing their functions on account of any activities performed by them in their official capacity. In the event, however, of an 'abuse of privileges committed . . . outside his official functions' the representative may be required to leave by the host Government 'in accordance with the diplomatic procedure applicable to diplomatic envoys accredited to that country'. Although no case law[3] has developed around the application of this section, it represents a satisfactory way of handling any instances which may arise from the standpoint of the member State, the host State and the international organization. Broadly similar provisions have been included in a number of conference and headquarters agreements. As the Sixth Committee emphasized when examining the relevant clauses of the Headquarters Agreement with the United States, it is essential that the powers so conferred are invoked only on serious grounds, so as to preclude the possibility of unwarranted accusations, and, secondly, that consultations should be held between the host authorities and the appropriate Government in the event that a demand is made for the departure of a particular representative.[4]

---

[1] Article IV, Section 14.   [2] Article VII, Section 24.

[3] See, however, the expulsion of a member of the ILO Governing Body discussed by Fischer, *Annuaire français de droit international* (1955), p. 385.

[4] *Report of the Sixth Committee*, A/427, 27 October 1947. See, generally, Gross, op. cit., at p. 508 *et seq.*

Appendix I

BIBLIOGRAPHICAL NOTE

A thorough bibliography of works relating to a subject as well studied as diplomatic relations and immunities might easily be as long as the body of present text. This note is merely intended to list some of the main sources of further information. There are two bibliographical studies which may be consulted. F. Moussa's *Diplomatie Contemporaine, Guide Bibliographique* (1964), while not dealing especially with the legal aspects of the subject, lists many publications of interest. Van Essen and Tichelaar, *Immunities in International Law* (Selective Bibliographies of the Library of the Peace Palace, III (1955)), covers works on diplomatic immunities and on the immunities of persons connected with international organizations. Besides these, Cahier, *Le Droit Diplomatique Contemporaine* (1962), contains a bibliographical section, as well as being in itself a good overall survey.

There are some thirty or more studies on the Vienna Convention. Amongst the best of these are those by Colliard, 'La Convention de Vienne sur les relations diplomatiques', *Annuaire français de droit international* (1961), p. 3, Kerley, 'Some aspects of the Vienna Conference on Diplomatic Intercourse and Immunities', *American Journal of International Law*, 56 (1962), p. 88, and Suy, 'La Convention de Vienne sur les relations diplomatiques', *Osterreichische Zeitschrift für öffentliches Recht*, 12 (1962), p. 86.

As regards international organizations, no magistral work has appeared. Jenks, *International Immunities* (1961), deals only shortly with the position of representatives. Gross, 'Immunities and Privileges of Delegations to the United Nations', *International Organization*, 16 (1962), p. 483, is an intricately argued assessment of the position at United Nations Headquarters. In the case of the European communities, amongst the many excellent studies which have been made in this context, two are outstanding: Pescatore, 'Les Relations extérieures des Communautés Européennes', *Académie de Droit International*, II (1961), p. 1, an illuminating series of lectures combining practical knowledge with conceptual imagination; and Salmon, *Les Représentations permanentes auprès de la C.E.E. et de l'Euratom* (1965), prepared for the study group on international organization organized by the European Centre of the Carnegie Endowment for International Peace.

Documentary sources are largely contained in two United Nations publications. National legislation on diplomatic privileges and immunities is to be found in United Nations Legislative Series, *Laws and Regulations regarding Diplomatic and Consular Privileges and Immunities*, VII (1958). International agreements and national laws relating to international organizations are collected in United Nations Legislative Series, *Legislative Texts and Treaty Provisions concerning the Legal Status, Privileges and Immunities of International Organizations*, volumes I and II (1959 and 1961). The *United Nations Juridical Yearbook*, which has appeared annually since 1962 (in 1962 in preliminary fascicle only) includes, *inter alia*, the text of national enactments and international agreements relating to the legal status of the United Nations and its associated bodies. Reference should also be made to the Secretariat study *The Practice of the United Nations, the Specialized Agencies and the International Atomic Energy Agency concerning their Status, Privileges and Immunities* (A/CN.4/L.118, 8 March 1967).

The proceedings of the Vienna Conference are contained in *United Nations Conference on Diplomatic Intercourse and Immunities, Official Records*, volumes I and II (1961 and 1962). The text of the Vienna Convention on Diplomatic Relations is reproduced in Appendix II.

Appendix II

VIENNA CONVENTION ON DIPLOMATIC RELATIONS

The Vienna Convention on Diplomatic Relations was adopted on 14 April 1961 at the end of the United Nations Conference on Diplomatic Intercourse and Immunities, held at the Neue Hofburg in Vienna between 2 March and 14 April 1961. The Convention entered into force on 24 April 1964. On 1 December 1967 the following sixty-five States were parties: Afghanistan, Algeria, Argentina, Austria, Brazil, Byelorussian SSR, Cambodia, Canada, Congo (Brazzaville), Democratic Republic of the Congo, Costa Rica, Cuba, Czechoslovakia, Dahomey, Dominican Republic, Ecuador, El Salvador, Federal Republic of Germany, Gabon, Ghana, Guatemala, Holy See, Hungary, India, Iran, Iraq, Ireland, Ivory Coast, Jamaica, Japan, Kenya, Laos, Liberia, Liechtenstein, Luxembourg, Madagascar, Malawi, Malaysia, Malta, Mauritania, Mexico, Mongolia, Nepal, Niger, Nigeria, Norway, Pakistan, Panama, Philippines, Poland, Rwanda, San Marino, Sierra Leone, Spain, Sweden, Switzerland, Tanzania, Trinidad, Uganda, Ukrainian SSR, USSR, United Arab Republic, United Kingdom, Venezuela and Yugoslavia.

In addition to the Convention, the Conference adopted an Optional Protocol concerning the Acquisition of Nationality,[1] which provides that members of missions shall not acquire the nationality of the receiving State solely by the operation of the laws of that State, and an Optional Protocol concerning the Compulsory Settlement of Disputes,[2] both of which came into force on 24 April 1964.

The text of the Convention[3] is reproduced below.

---

[1] *United Nations Treaty Series*, vol. 500, p. 223. On 1 December 1967 the following twenty-one States were parties to the Optional Protocol: Argentina, Cambodia, Dominican Republic, Federal Republic of Germany, Gabon, India, Iran, Iraq, Kenya, Laos, Madagascar, Malaysia, Nepal, Niger, Norway, Panama, Philippines, Sweden, Tanzania, United Arab Republic and Yugoslavia.

[2] Idem, p. 241. On 1 December 1967 the following twenty-nine States were parties to the Optional Protocol: Austria, Cambodia, Democratic Republic of Congo, Costa Rica, Dominican Republic, Ecuador, Federal Republic of Germany, Gabon, India, Iran, Iraq, Japan, Kenya, Laos, Liechtenstein, Luxembourg, Madagascar, Malaysia, Malta, Nepal, Niger, Norway, Panama, Philippines, Sweden, Switzerland, Tanzania, United Kingdom and Yugoslavia.

[3] Idem, p. 95. The reservations or declarations made with reference to Article 8, paragraph 3, Article 11, paragraph 1, Article 34(a), Article 37, paragraph 2, and Article 38, have been noted in the text. (See pp. 29, 30, 71, 76 and 79 above.) Declarations were made regarding Articles 48 and 50 by Byelorussian SSR, Cuba (objected to by Guatemala), Hungary (objected to by Luxembourg), Mongolia, Ukrainian SSR and USSR.

For the text of declarations or reservations, and the statements of other States parties with regard to them, see *Multilateral Treaties in respect of which the Secretary-General performs depositary functions* (ST/LEG/SER.D/1).

VIENNA CONVENTION ON DIPLOMATIC RELATIONS. DONE AT VIENNA, ON 18 APRIL 1961

The States Parties to the present Convention,

Recalling that peoples of all nations from ancient times have recognized the status of diplomatic agents,

Having in mind the purposes and principles of the Charter of the United Nations concerning the sovereign equality of States, the maintenance of international peace and security, and the promotion of friendly relations among nations,

Believing that an international convention on diplomatic intercourse, privileges and immunities would contribute to the development of friendly relations among nations, irrespective of their differing constitutional and social systems,

Realizing that the purpose of such privileges and immunities is not to benefit individuals but to ensure the efficient performance of the functions of diplomatic missions as representing States,

Affirming that the rules of customary international law should continue to govern questions not expressly regulated by the provisions of the present Convention,

Have agreed as follows:

Article 1

For the purpose of the present Convention, the following expressions shall have the meanings hereunder assigned to them:

(a) the 'head of the mission' is the person charged by the sending State with the duty of acting in that capacity;

(b) the 'members of the mission' are the head of the mission and the members of the staff of the mission;

(c) the 'members of the staff of the mission' are the members of the diplomatic staff, of the administrative and technical staff and of the service staff of the mission;

(d) the 'members of the diplomatic staff' are the members of the staff of the mission having diplomatic rank;

(e) a 'diplomatic agent' is the head of the mission or a member of the diplomatic staff of the mission;

(f) the 'members of the administrative and technical staff' are the members of the staff of the mission employed in the administrative and technical service of the mission;

(g) the 'members of the service staff' are the members of the staff of the mission in the domestic service of the mission;

(h) a 'private servant' is a person who is in the domestic service of a member of the mission and who is not an employee of the sending State;

(i) the 'premises of the mission' are the buildings or parts of buildings and the land ancillary thereto, irrespective of ownership, used for the purposes of the mission including the residence of the head of the mission.

Article 2

The establishment of diplomatic relations between States, and of permanent diplomatic missions, takes place by mutual consent.

Article 3

1. The functions of a diplomatic mission consist *inter alia* in:
(*a*) representing the sending State in the receiving State;
(*b*) protecting in the receiving State the interests of the sending State and of its nationals, within the limits permitted by international law;
(*c*) negotiating with the Government of the receiving State;
(*d*) ascertaining by all lawful means conditions and developments in the receiving State, and reporting thereon to the Government of the sending State;
(*e*) promoting friendly relations between the sending State and the receiving State, and developing their economic, cultural and scientific relations.

2. Nothing in the present Convention shall be construed as preventing the performance of consular functions by a diplomatic mission.

Article 4

1. The sending State must make certain that the *agrément* of the receiving State has been given for the person it proposes to accredit as head of the mission to that State.

2. The receiving State is not obliged to give reasons to the sending State for a refusal of *agrément*.

Article 5

1. The sending State may, after it has given due notification to the receiving States concerned, accredit a head of mission or assign any member of the diplomatic staff, as the case may be, to more than one State, unless there is express objection by any of the receiving States.

2. If the sending State accredits a head of mission to one or more other States it may establish a diplomatic mission headed by a chargé d'affaires ad interim in each State where the head of mission has not his permanent seat.

3. A head of mission or any member of the diplomatic staff of the mission may act as representative of the sending State to any international organization.

APPENDIX II

Article 6

Two or more States may accredit the same person as head of mission to another State, unless objection is offered by the receiving State.

Article 7

Subject to the provisions of Articles 5, 8, 9, and 11, the sending State may freely appoint the members of the staff of the mission. In the case of military, naval or air attachés, the receiving State may require their names to be submitted beforehand, for its approval.

Article 8

1. Members of the diplomatic staff of the mission should in principle be of the nationality of the sending State.
2. Members of the diplomatic staff of the mission may not be appointed from among persons having the nationality of the receiving State, except with the consent of that State which may be withdrawn at any time.
3. The receiving State may reserve the same right with regard to nationals of a third State who are not also nationals of the sending State.

Article 9

1. The receiving State may at any time and without having to explain its decision, notify the sending State that the head of the mission or any member of the diplomatic staff of the mission is *persona non grata* or that any other member of the staff of the mission is not acceptable. In any such case, the sending State shall, as appropriate, either recall the person concerned or terminate his functions with the mission. A person may be declared *non grata* or not acceptable before arriving in the territory of the receiving State.
2. If the sending State refuses or fails within a reasonable period to carry out its obligations under paragraph 1 of this Article, the receiving State may refuse to recognize the person concerned as a member of the mission.

Article 10

1. The Ministry for Foreign Affairs of the receiving State, or such other ministry as may be agreed, shall be notified of:
(a) the appointment of members of the mission, their arrival and their final departure or the termination of their functions with the mission;
(b) the arrival and final departure of a person belonging to the family of a member of the mission and, where appropriate, the fact that a person becomes or ceases to be a member of the family of a member of the mission;
(c) the arrival and final departure of private servants in the employ of persons referred to in sub-paragraph (a) of this paragraph and, where appropriate, the fact that they are leaving the employ of such persons;

132

(*d*) the engagement and discharge of persons resident in the receiving State as members of the mission or private servants entitled to privileges and immunities.

2. Where possible, prior notification of arrival and final departure shall also be given.

Article 11

1. In the absence of specific agreement as to the size of the mission, the receiving State may require that the size of a mission be kept within limits considered by it to be reasonable and normal, having regard to circumstances and conditions in the receiving State and to the needs of the particular mission.

2. The receiving State may equally, within similar bounds and on a non-discriminatory basis, refuse to accept officials of a particular category.

Article 12

The sending State may not, without the prior express consent of the receiving State, establish offices forming part of the mission in localities other than those in which the mission itself is established.

Article 13

1. The head of the mission is considered as having taken up his functions in the receiving State either when he has presented his credentials or when he has notified his arrival and a true copy of his credentials has been presented to the Ministry for Foreign Affairs of the receiving State, or such other ministry as may be agreed, in accordance with the practice prevailing in the receiving State which shall be applied in a uniform manner.

2. The order of presentation of credentials or of a true copy thereof will be determined by the date and time of the arrival of the head of the mission.

Article 14

1. Heads of mission are divided into three classes, namely:

(*a*) that of ambassadors or nuncios accredited to Heads of State, and other heads of mission of equivalent rank;
(*b*) that of envoys, ministers and internuncios accredited to Heads of State;
(*c*) that of chargés d'affaires accredited to Ministers for Foreign Affairs.

2. Except as concerns precedence and etiquette, there shall be no differentiation between heads of mission by reason of their class.

Article 15

The class to which the heads of their missions are to be assigned shall be agreed between States.

Article 16

1. Heads of mission shall take precedence in their respective classes in the order of the date and time of taking up their functions in accordance with Article 13.

2. Alterations in the credentials of a head of mission not involving any change of class shall not affect his precedence.

3. This article is without prejudice to any practice accepted by the receiving State regarding the precedence of the representative of the Holy See.

Article 17

The precedence of the members of the diplomatic staff of the mission shall be notified by the head of the mission to the Ministry for Foreign Affairs or such other ministry as may be agreed.

Article 18

The procedure to be observed in each State for the reception of heads of mission shall be uniform in respect of each class.

Article 19

1. If the post of head of the mission is vacant, or if the head of the mission is unable to perform his functions, a chargé d'affaires ad interim shall act provisionally as head of the mission. The name of the chargé d'affaires ad interim shall be notified, either by the head of the mission or, in case he is unable to do so, by the Ministry for Foreign Affairs of the sending State to the Ministry for Foreign Affairs of the receiving State or such other ministry as may be agreed.

2. In cases where no member of the diplomatic staff of the mission is present in the receiving State, a member of the administrative and technical staff may, with the consent of the receiving State, be designated by the sending State to be in charge of the current administrative affairs of the mission.

Article 20

The mission and its head shall have the right to use the flag and emblem of the sending State on the premises of the mission, including the residence of the head of the mission, and on his means of transport.

Article 21

1. The receiving State shall either facilitate the acquisition on its territory, in accordance with its laws, by the sending State of premises necessary for its mission or assist the latter in obtaining accommodation in some other way.

2. It shall also, where necessary, assist missions in obtaining suitable accommodation for their members.

Article 22

1. The premises of the mission shall be inviolable. The agents of the receiving State may not enter them, except with the consent of the head of the mission.

2. The receiving State is under a special duty to take all appropriate steps to protect the premises of the mission against any intrusion or damage and to prevent any disturbance of the peace of the mission or impairment of its dignity.

3. The premises of the mission, their furnishings and other property thereon and the means of transport of the mission shall be immune from search, requisition, attachment or execution.

Article 23

1. The sending State and the head of the mission shall be exempt from all national, regional or municipal dues and taxes in respect of the premises of the mission, whether owned or leased, other than such as represent payment for specific services rendered.

2. The exemption from taxation referred to in this Article shall not apply to such dues and taxes payable under the law of the receiving State by persons contracting with the sending State or the head of the mission.

Article 24

The archives and documents of the mission shall be inviolable at any time and wherever they may be.

Article 25

The receiving State shall accord full facilities for the performance of the functions of the mission.

Article 26

Subject to its laws and regulations concerning zones entry into which is prohibited or regulated for reasons of national security, the receiving State shall ensure to all members of the mission freedom of movement and travel in its territory.

Article 27

1. The receiving State shall permit and protect free communication on the part of the mission for all official purposes. In communicating with the Government and the other missions and consulates of the sending State, wherever situated, the mission may employ all appropriate means,

including diplomatic couriers and messages in code or cipher. However, the mission may install and use a wireless transmitter only with the consent of the receiving State.

2. The official correspondence of the mission shall be inviolable. Official correspondence means all correspondence relating to the mission and its functions.

3. The diplomatic bag shall not be opened or detained.

4. The packages constituting the diplomatic bag must bear visible external marks of their character and may contain only diplomatic documents or articles intended for official use.

5. The diplomatic courier, who shall be provided with an official document indicating his status and the number of packages constituting the diplomatic bag, shall be protected by the receiving State in the performance of his functions. He shall enjoy personal inviolability and shall not be liable to any form of arrest or detention.

6. The sending State or the mission may designate diplomatic couriers *ad hoc*. In such cases the provisions of paragraph 5 of this Article shall also apply, except that the immunities therein mentioned shall cease to apply when such a courier has delivered to the consignee the diplomatic bag in his charge.

7. A diplomatic bag may be entrusted to the captain of a commercial aircraft scheduled to land at an authorized port of entry. He shall be provided with an official document indicating the number of packages constituting the bag but he shall not be considered to be a diplomatic courier. The mission may send one of its members to take possession of the diplomatic bag directly and freely from the captain of the aircraft.

Article 28

The fees and charges levied by the mission in the course of its official duties shall be exempt from all dues and taxes.

Article 29

The person of a diplomatic agent shall be inviolable. He shall not be liable to any form of arrest or detention. The receiving State shall treat him with due respect and shall take all appropriate steps to prevent any attack on his person, freedom or dignity.

Article 30

1. The private residence of a diplomatic agent shall enjoy the same inviolability and protection as the premises of the mission.

2. His papers, correspondence and, except as provided in paragraph 3 of Article 31, his property, shall likewise enjoy inviolability.

Article 31

1. A diplomatic agent shall enjoy immunity from the criminal jurisdiction of the receiving State. He shall also enjoy immunity from its civil and administrative jurisdiction, except in the case of:

(a) a real action relating to private immovable property situated in the territory of the receiving State, unless he holds it on behalf of the sending State for the purposes of the mission;

(b) an action relating to succession in which the diplomatic agent is involved as executor, administrator, heir or legatee as a private person and not on behalf of the sending State;

(c) an action relating to any professional or commercial activity exercised by the diplomatic agent in the receiving State outside his official functions.

2. A diplomatic agent is not obliged to give evidence as a witness.

3. No measures of execution may be taken in respect of a diplomatic agent except in the cases coming under sub-paragraphs (a), (b) and (c) of paragraph 1 of this Article, and provided that the measures concerned can be taken without infringing the inviolability of his person or of his residence.

4. The immunity of a diplomatic agent from the jurisdiction of the receiving State does not exempt him from the jurisdiction of the sending State.

Article 32

1. The immunity from jurisdiction of diplomatic agents and of persons enjoying immunity under Article 37 may be waived by the sending State.

2. Waiver must always be express.

3. The initiation of proceedings by a diplomatic agent or by a person enjoying immunity from jurisdiction under Article 37 shall preclude him from invoking immunity from jurisdiction in respect of any counter-claim directly connected with the principal claim.

4. Waiver of immunity from jurisdiction in respect of civil or administrative proceedings shall not be held to imply waiver of immunity in respect of the execution of the judgment, for which a separate waiver shall be necessary.

Article 33

1. Subject to the provisions of paragraph 3 of this Article, a diplomatic agent shall with respect to services rendered for the sending State be exempt from social security provisions which may be in force in the receiving State.

2. The exemption provided for in paragraph 1 of this Article shall also apply to private servants who are in the sole employ of a diplomatic agent, on condition:

(a) that they are not nationals of or permanently resident in the receiving State; and (*b*) that they are covered by the social security provisions which may be in force in the sending State or a third State.

3. A diplomatic agent who employs persons to whom the exemption provided for in paragraph 2 of this Article does not apply shall observe the obligations which the social security provisions of the receiving State impose upon employers.

4. The exemption provided for in paragraphs 1 and 2 of this Article shall not preclude voluntary participation in the social security system of the receiving State provided that such participation is permitted by that State.

5. The provisions of this Article shall not affect bilateral or multilateral agreements concerning social security concluded previously and shall not prevent the conclusion of such agreements in the future.

Article 34

A diplomatic agent shall be exempt from all dues and taxes, personal or real, national, regional or municipal, except:

(*a*) indirect taxes of a kind which are normally incorporated in the price of goods or services;

(*b*) dues and taxes on private immovable property situated in the territory of the receiving State, unless he holds it on behalf of the sending State for the purposes of the mission;

(*c*) estate, succession or inheritance duties levied by the receiving State, subject to the provisions of paragraph 4 of Article 39;

(*d*) dues and taxes on private income having its source in the receiving State and capital taxes on investments made in commercial undertakings in the receiving State;

(*e*) charges levied for specific services rendered;

(*f*) registration, court or record fees, mortgage dues and stamp duty, with respect to immovable property, subject to the provisions of Article 23.

Article 35

The receiving State shall exempt diplomatic agents from all personal services, from all public service of any kind whatsoever, and from military obligations such as those connected with requisitioning, military contributions and billeting.

Article 36

1. The receiving State shall, in accordance with such laws and regulations as it may adopt, permit entry of and grant exemption from all customs duties, taxes, and related charges other than charges for storage, cartage and similar services, on:

(*a*) articles for the official use of the mission;

(*b*) articles for the personal use of a diplomatic agent or members of his family forming part of his household, including articles intended for his establishment.

138

2. The personal baggage of a diplomatic agent shall be exempt from inspection, unless there are serious grounds for presuming that it contains articles not covered by the exemptions mentioned in paragraph 1 of this Article, or articles the import or export of which is prohibited by the law or controlled by the quarantine regulations of the receiving State. Such inspection shall be conducted only in the presence of the diplomatic agent or of his authorized representative.

Article 37

1. The members of the family of a diplomatic agent forming part of his household shall, if they are not nationals of the receiving State, enjoy the privileges and immunities specified in Articles 29 to 36.

2. Members of the administrative and technical staff of the mission, together with members of their families forming part of their respective households, shall, if they are not nationals of or permanently resident in the receiving State, enjoy the privileges and immunities specified in Articles 29 to 35, except that the immunity from civil and administrative jurisdiction of the receiving State specified in paragraph 1 of Article 31 shall not extend to acts performed outside the course of their duties. They shall also enjoy the privileges specified in Article 36, paragraph 1, in respect of articles imported at the time of first installation.

3. Members of the service staff of the mission who are not nationals of or permanently resident in the receiving State shall enjoy immunity in respect of acts performed in the course of their duties, exemption from dues and taxes on the emoluments they receive by reason of their employment and the exemption contained in Article 33.

4. Private servants of members of the mission shall, if they are not nationals of or permanently resident in the receiving State, be exempt from dues and taxes on the emoluments they receive by reason of their employment. In other respects, they may enjoy privileges and immunities only to the extent admitted by the receiving State. However, the receiving State must exercise its jurisdiction over those persons in such a manner as not to interfere unduly with the performance of the functions of the mission.

Article 38

1. Except insofar as additional privileges and immunities may be granted by the receiving State, a diplomatic agent who is a national of or permanently resident in that State shall enjoy only immunity from jurisdiction, and inviolability, in respect of official acts performed in the exercise of his functions.

2. Other members of the staff of the mission and private servants who are nationals of or permanently resident in the receiving State shall enjoy privileges and immunities only to the extent admitted by the receiving State. However, the receiving State must exercise its jurisdiction over those persons in such a manner as not to interfere unduly with the performance of the functions of the mission.

Article 39

1. Every person entitled to privileges and immunities shall enjoy them from the moment he enters the territory of the receiving State on proceeding to take up his post or, if already in its territory, from the moment when his appointment is notified to the Ministry for Foreign Affairs or such other ministry as may be agreed.

2. When the functions of a person enjoying privileges and immunities have come to an end, such privileges and immunities shall normally cease at the moment when he leaves the country, or on expiry of a reasonable period in which to do so, but shall subsist until that time, even in case of armed conflict. However, with respect to acts performed by such a person in the exercise of his functions as a member of the mission, immunity shall continue to subsist.

3. In case of the death of a member of the mission, the members of his family shall continue to enjoy the privileges and immunities to which they are entitled until the expiry of a reasonable period in which to leave the country.

4. In the event of the death of a member of the mission not a national of or permanently resident in the receiving State or a member of his family forming part of his household, the receiving State shall permit the withdrawal of the movable property of the deceased, with the exception of any property acquired in the country the export of which was prohibited at the time of his death. Estate, succession and inheritance duties shall not be levied on movable property the presence of which in the receiving State was due solely to the presence there of the deceased as a member of the mission or as a member of the family of a member of the mission.

Article 40

1. If a diplomatic agent passes through or is in the territory of a third State, which has granted him a passport visa if such visa was necessary, while proceeding to take up or to return to his post, or when returning to his own country, the third State shall accord him inviolability and such other immunities as may be required to ensure his transit or return. The same shall apply in the case of any members of his family enjoying privileges or immunities who are accompanying the diplomatic agent, or travelling separately to join him or to return to their country.

2. In circumstances similar to those specified in paragraph 1 of this Article, third States shall not hinder the passage of members of the administrative and technical or service staff of a mission, and of members of their families, through their territories.

3. Third States shall accord to official correspondence and other official communications in transit, including messages in code or cipher, the same freedom and protection as is accorded by the receiving State. They shall accord to diplomatic couriers, who have been granted a passport visa if such visa was necessary, and diplomatic bags in transit the same inviolability and protection as the receiving State is bound to accord.

4. The obligations of third States under paragraphs 1, 2 and 3 of this

Article shall also apply to the persons mentioned respectively in those paragraphs, and to official communications and diplomatic bags, whose presence in the territory of the third State is due to *force majeure*.

Article 41

1. Without prejudice to their privileges and immunities, it is the duty of all persons enjoying such privileges and immunities to respect the laws and regulations of the receiving State. They also have a duty not to interfere in the internal affairs of that State.

2. All official business with the receiving State entrusted to the mission by the sending State shall be conducted with or through the Ministry for Foreign Affairs of the receiving State or such other ministry as may be agreed.

3. The premises of the mission must not be used in any manner incompatible with the functions of the mission as laid down in the present Convention or by other rules of general international law or by any special agreements in force between the sending and the receiving State.

Article 42

A diplomatic agent shall not in the receiving State practise for personal profit any professional or commercial activity.

Article 43

The function of a diplomatic agent comes to an end, *inter alia*:

(a) on notification by the sending State to the receiving State that the function of the diplomatic agent has come to an end;

(b) on notification by the receiving State to the sending State that, in accordance with paragraph 2 of Article 9, it refuses to recognize the diplomatic agent as a member of the mission.

Article 44

The receiving State must, even in case of armed conflict, grant facilities in order to enable persons enjoying privileges and immunities, other than nationals of the receiving State, and members of the families of such persons irrespective of their nationality, to leave at the earliest possible moment. It must, in particular, in case of need, place at their disposal the necessary means of transport for themselves and their property.

Article 45

If diplomatic relations are broken off between two States, or if a mission is permanently or temporarily recalled:

(a) The receiving State must, even in case of armed conflict, respect and protect the premises of the mission, together with its property and archives;

(b) the sending State may entrust the custody of the premises of the mission, together with its property and archives, to a third State acceptable to the receiving State;

(c) the sending State may entrust the protection of its interests and those of its nationals to a third State acceptable to the receiving State.

Article 46

A sending State may with the prior consent of a receiving State, and at the request of a third State not represented in the receiving State, undertake the temporary protection of the interests of the third State and of its nationals.

Article 47

1. In the application of the provisions of the present Convention, the receiving State shall not discriminate as between States.

2. However, discrimination shall not be regarded as taking place:

(a) where the receiving State applies any of the provisions of the present Convention restrictively because of a restrictive application of that provision to its mission in the sending State;

(b) where by custom or agreement States extend to each other more favourable treatment than is required by the provisions of the present Convention.

Article 48

The present Convention shall be open for signature by all States Members of the United Nations or of any of the specialized agencies or Parties to the Statute of the International Court of Justice, and by any other State invited by the General Assembly of the United Nations to become a Party to the Convention, as follows: until 31 October 1961 at the Federal Ministry for Foreign Affairs of Austria and subsequently, until 31 March 1962, at the United Nations Headquarters in New York.

Article 49

The present Convention is subject to ratification. The instruments of ratification shall be deposited with the Secretary-General of the United Nations.

Article 50

The present Convention shall remain open for accession by any State belonging to any of the four categories mentioned in Article 48. The instruments of accession shall be deposited with the Secretary-General of the United Nations.

Article 51

1. The present Convention shall enter into force on the thirtieth day following the date of deposit of the twenty-second instrument of ratification or accession with the Secretary-General of the United Nations.

2. For each State ratifying or acceding to the Convention after the deposit of the twenty-second instrument of ratification or accession, the Convention shall enter into force on the thirtieth day after deposit by such State of its instrument of ratification or accession.

Article 52

The Secretary-General of the United Nations shall inform all States belonging to any of the four categories mentioned in Article 48:

(a) of signatures to the present Convention and of the deposit of instruments of ratification or accession, in accordance with Articles 48, 49 and 50;

(b) of the date on which the present Convention will enter into force, in accordance with Article 51.

Article 53

The original of the present Convention, of which the Chinese, English, French, Russian and Spanish texts are equally authentic, shall be deposited with the Secretary-General of the United Nations, who shall send certified copies thereof to all States belonging to any of the four categories mentioned in Article 48.

IN WITNESS WHEREOF the undersigned Plenipotentiaries, being duly authorized thereto by their respective Governments, have signed the present Convention.

DONE at Vienna, this eighteenth day of April one thousand nine hundred and sixty-one.

INDEX

Act of Anne, 1708, 52n., 58–9, 64, 81
Afghanistan, 129
Agrément, 19–21, 25, 102–4, 106
Albania, 13n.
Algeria, 129
Arab League, 95, 100n.
Argentina, 30, 45n., 129
Austria, 62n., 72n., 74n., 95n., 123, 129

Bartoš, 39n., 76n.; *see also* International Law Commission (*b*) Special Missions, Special Rapporteur
Belgium, 87n., 95n., 116, 117n., 120
Bentham, 4
Beyen, 2n.
Blix, 18n.
Bowett, 7n.
Braunas and Stourzh, 2n.
Brazil, 129
Bulgaria, 13n., 85n., 87
Byelorussian SSR, 30n., 129

Cahier, 127
Cambodia, 76n., 129
Cameroons, 24n.
Canada, 30n., 49n., 95n., 129
Cardozo, 54n.
Cases:
  Afghan Embassy, 48n.
  Amazone, 50
  Arcaya *v.* Paez, 81–2
  Asylum, 5
  B. *v.* M., 26n., 115
  Bergman *v.* De Sieyès, 88n.
  Charkieh, 56n.
  'Corfu Incident', 52
  Dickinson *v.* Del Solar, 53
  Empson *v.* Smith, 64n., 82
  Engelke *v.* Musmann, 54n.

Ghosh *v.* D'Rozario, 81–2
In re De la Baume, 19n.
In re Ledoux, 50n.
In re Vitianu, 26
Ivory Coast–Guinea dispute, 88n., 123
Leslie, Bishop of Ross, 57n.
Macartney *v.* Garbett, 79n.
Magdalena Steam Navigation Co. *v.* Martin, 82n.
Marche's Case, 57n.
Pappas *v.* Francini, 114n.
Petrocchino *v.* Swedish State, 43n.
Procureur général c. Nazare Aga, 81n.
R. *v.* Kent, 83n.
R. *v.* Rose, 49n.
Re Nijdam, 62n.
Respublica *v.* de Longchamps, 52n.
Re Suarez, 83n.
Romanian Legation in Berne, 47–8
Salm *v.* Frazier, 55n.
Santiesteban Case, 26n., 112–14
Sun Yat Sen Case, 44n.
Triquet *v.* Bath, 58n.
Zoernsch *v.* Waldock, 65n.
Central African Republic, 24n.
Certificate of the Executive, 54, 59, 65
Chad, 24n.
Chalfont, Lord, 90
Chargé d'affaires, *see* Staff of diplomatic missions
Chile, 95n.
China, 35n., 44n., 46n., 120, 121–122
Cohen, 49n.
Colliard, 23n., 127
Colombia, 43

144

France, 13n., 18n., 19n., 23n., 24, 27, 28n., 38, 39n., 44n., 45n., 54, 57, 87n., 95n., 121–2
Franchise de l'hôtel, 41
Franchise de quartier, 41n.
François, 34n.
Freedom of communication, 36–40
Freedom of movement, 32, 34–5, 118–19
French Community, 23n.

Gabon, 24n., 129
Germany, Federal Republic of, 30n., 34n., 38n., 76n., 87n., 102, 129
Ghana, 45n., 129
Goy, 125n.
Greece, 13n., 76n., 105
Gross, 124n., 126n., 127
Grotius, 9, 57
Guatemala, 129
Guinea, 88n., 123

Hadwen and Kaufmann, 101n.
Hale, Sir Matthew, 57
Harvard Law School, Research in International Law, I: Diplomatic Privileges and Immunities, 5–6, 78n.
Hasluck, 90
Havana Convention regarding Diplomatic Officers, 5–6
Head of Mission, *see* Staff of diplomatic missions
Holy See, 2, 23, 24, 102, 129; papal nuncios and internuncios, 22–3
Hoppenot, 101n.
Houben, 99n.
Hungary, 85n., 87, 129
Hurst, 57–8
Hyde, 14n.

Immunity from personal services, 73–4
India, 129
Indirect taxes, 71
Indonesia, 46n., 87n.
Inspection of personal baggage, 73, 109

Inter-governmental Maritime Consultative Organization (IMCO), 95n.
International Atomic Energy Agency (IAEA), 95n., 122–123
International Bank for Reconstruction and Development (IBRD), 95n., 99
International Civil Aviation Organization (ICAO), 95n.
International Court of Justice, 95n., 126
International Development Association (IDA), 95n.
International Finance Corporation (IFC), 95n.
International Labour Organization (ILO), 95n., 97–9, 126n.
International Law Commission
(*a*) Diplomatic Relations
— Special Rapporteur (Mr A. E. F. Sandström (Sweden)) 6n., 13n., 69n.
— *Yearbooks of the International Law Commission: 1955, II*, 6n., 13n., 22n., 69n.; *1956, II*, 5; *1957, I*, 6n., 25n., 26n., 33n., 34n., 39n., 42n., 61n., 76n., 88n.; *1957, II*, 22n., 61n., 73n.; *1958, I*, 23n., 33n., 34n., 88n.; *1958, II*, 5n., 6n., 10n., 22n., 33n., 36n., 40n., 44n., 45n., 46n., 50n., 58n., 64n., 67n., 70n., 75n., 84n.
(*b*) Special Missions
— Report of the International Law Commission on the Work of its Nineteenth Session, 1967, 25n., 61n., 91–4
— Special Rapporteur (Mr M. Bartoš (Yugoslavia)), 91
— *Yearbooks of the International Law Commission, 1963, II*, 91n.; *1964, II*, 91n., *1965, II*, 91n.

International Monetary Fund (IMF), 95n., 99n.
International Telecommunications Union (ITU), 95n.
Inviolability: archives and documents, 49; correspondence, 39; papers, 109; personal, 50–2, 75; premises, 8–9, 41–8, 121–2; property, 48–50, 68n.; residence, 43, 85
Iran, 115, 129
Iraq, 76n., 129
Ireland, 28n., 79n., 129
Israel, 34n., 37n., 61, 95n., 124
Italy, 2, 24n., 28n., 81n.
Ivory Coast, 88n., 123, 129

Jackson, 82n.
Jamaica, 129
Japan, 45, 71n., 129
Jenks, 127
Jervis on the Office and Duties of Coroners, 83n.
Jones, 82n.
Jurisdictional immunity, 8–10, 52–68, 75, 85, 118
— Immunity from civil and administrative jurisdiction, 58–61, 88; exceptions, 61–2, 72; resolution on civil claims, 61
— Immunity from criminal jurisdiction and arrest, 48n., 51, 56–8, 86n., 88, 108, 112–13
— Immunity from giving evidence, 67
— Immunity in respect of acts performed in the exercise of official functions, 64–7, 79, 83, 85, 108–9, 110n., 118, 126

Kenya, 129
Kerley, 38n., 127
Kiss, 18n., 38n., 42n., 44n., 54n., 60n., 81n.
Korea, Republic of, 102

Laos, 129
Lauterpacht, 18n., 35n., 60n., 65n., 86n.

League of Nations, 5, 10, 14n., 52n., 119
Liang, 102n.
Liberia, 129
Liechtenstein, 129
Louis-Lucas, 47n., 48n.
Luxembourg, 30n., 87n., 95n., 116, 117n., 129
Lyons, 48n., 52n., 54n., 83n.

Madagascar, 129
Mansfield, Lord, 58n.
Malawi, 129
Malaysia, 129
Malta, 30n., 76n., 129
Martens, 23n.
Mattingly, 36n., 41n.
Mauritania, 129
McNair, Lord, 44n., 57n.
Mexico, 129
Mill, J. S., 1
Monaco, 102
Mongolia, 30n., 129
Montesquieu, 11
Moore, 48n.
Moussa, 127

Nationals, or permanent residents, of the receiving State, 28–9, 65, 75, 78–80, 81, 86
Nepal, 29n., 129
Nervo, Padilla, 43n.
Netherlands, 34, 59, 60–1, 62n., 87n., 95n.
Niboyet, 67n.
Niger, 129
Nigeria, 38n., 129
Noel, 99n.
Non-discrimination and reciprocity, 30, 35, 75, 83–7, 93–4, 117–19
North Atlantic Treaty Organization (NATO), 100n.
Norway, 45n., 55n., 129

Oppenheim, 52n.
Organization of African Unity (OAU), 95, 100n.
Organization of American States (OAS), 95, 100n.

Pakistan, 124

Panama, 129

Permanent representatives and missions, 100–1, 103–5, 109–10, 114–116, 118, 120

Perrenoud, 35n.

Perrin, 47n., 48n.

Persona non grata or 'not acceptable' procedure, 8, 20, 27, 31–2, 56, 58, 61n., 110, 125

Pescatore, 127

Philippines, 129

Phillimore, Lord, 54

Phillimore, Sir R., 56

Poland, 87n., 129

Portugal, 46n.

Precedence, 21–4

Premises: 9; acquisition or obtaining, 33; protection, 46–8; *see also* Fiscal and parafiscal immunities, Inviolability, and Jurisdictional immunity

Professional and commercial activities, 59, 62

Protocol of Aix-la-Chapelle, 22–3

Raton, 43n.

Reciprocity, *see* Non-discrimination

'Right of legation', 13–14

Romania, 26, 47–8

Romberg, 43n.

Rwanda, 129

Salmon, 22n, 82n., 105n., 116n., 127

Sandström, *see* International Law Commission (*a*) Diplomatic Relations, Special Rapporteur

San Marino, 129

Satow, 79n., 89

Savigny, 104

Sen, 2n.

Sierra Leone, 129

Simmonds, 9n.

Social security, 73–4, 77–8

Spain, 36n., 45n., 129

Special missions, 2–4, 25n., 61n., 62n., 89–94

Specialized Agencies, 2, 114n.; *see* *also* Convention on Privileges and Immunities of the Specialized Agencies, and under the title of individual agencies

Staff of diplomatic missions, 92
— Administrative and technical staff, 19, 65, 75–8; *see also* 85–87, 89
— Chargé d'affaires, 21–3; ad interim, 21
— Diplomatic agents, 19, 74–80
— Head of mission, 19, 20, 64, 72n., 81; classes and precedence, 21–4
— Members of family of staff, 62, 74, 77, 80, 81, 83n., 85–6, 89
— Private servants of staff, 74, 78, 80–1, 85–6
— Service attachés, 25, 27–8, 81
— Service staff, 19, 65, 75, 77; *see also* 86–7, 89

Stephen, 52n.

Stowell, 47n.

Suy, 127

Sweden, 129

Switzerland, 6n., 23n., 24, 26–8, 34n., 47–8, 60–1, 81, 95n., 102, 109, 114, 115, 119, 124n., 129

Tanzania, 30n., 129

Temporal limitation of privileges and immunities, *see* Duration of privileges and immunities

Thailand, 95n.

Thibault, 104

Transit, 87–9, 122–5

Trinidad, 129

Tunisia, 13n.

Tunkin, 11n., 25–7

Turkey, 45n., 105

Uganda, 129

Ukrainian SSR, 30n., 129

Union africaine et malgache, 25

USSR, 11n., 13n., 14n., 27, 35n., 39, 44n., 45n., 46n., 49n., 69n., 85n., 86n., 87, 99n., 108n., 129

United Arab Republic, 76n., 95n., 124, 129